Everyday Grammar

5770 4900

John Seely is an experienced author specializing in language and communication skills who has worked in education at all levels from primary school to university. His publications include the *Oxford English Programme* and the *Oxford Guide to Writing and Speaking*. He is also general editor of the *One Step Ahead* series.

Oxford Paperback Reference

The most authoritative and up-to-date reference books for both students and the general reader.

*forthcoming

Everyday Grammar

JOHN SEELY

OXFORD
UNIVERSITY PRESS

OXFORD

UNIVERSITY PRESS

Great Clarendon Street, Oxford OX2 6DP
Oxford University Press is a department of the University of Oxford.
It furthers the University's objective of excellence in research, scholarship,
and education by publishing worldwide in

Oxford New York

Auckland Bangkok Buenos Aires Cape Town Chennai
Dar es Salaam Delhi Hong Kong Istanbul Karachi Kolkata
Kuala Lumpur Madrid Melbourne Mexico City Mumbai Nairobi
São Paulo Shanghai Taipei Tokyo Toronto

Oxford is a registered trade mark of Oxford University Press
in the UK and certain other countries

Published in the United States
by Oxford University Press Inc., New York

British Library Cataloguing in Publication Data
Data available

Library of Congress Cataloging in Publication Data
Data available

ISBN 0-19-860874-8

3

Typeset in Swift and Frutiger
by Kolam Information Services Pvt. Ltd
Pondicherry, India
Printed in Great Britain by
Clays Ltd, St Ives plc

Acknowledgements

A work of popularisation such as this depends on a wide range of different sources, but I should like to acknowledge a particular debt to *The Oxford English Grammar* by the late Sidney Greenbaum. I have been greatly assisted by the kind but determined and detailed comments of Edmund Weiner at the different stages of the preparation of the text. He will know where his advice has been heeded (most of the time) or set aside (occasionally). Responsibility for the final text is, of course, mine alone.

I am also grateful for the comments and suggestions of my wife, Elizabeth, and for the valued support of Alysoun Owen and her colleagues at Oxford University Press.

I am always interested to receive comments and suggestions for improvements to the text. I can be contacted by email at grammar@yourenglish.com.

John Seely

Contents

Section A
Chapter 1:
Introduction

Topics in this chapter include:

- **problems encountered when studying grammar**
- **grammatical levels**
  Morphemes
  Words
  Phrases
  Clauses
  Sentences

Learning about Grammar

If you know absolutely nothing about grammar, the task of beginning to understand how it works can seem very daunting indeed. (If it's any consolation, the task of explaining it feels quite daunting, too!) Fortunately it is very rare for a person to 'know absolutely nothing about grammar', even if you feel that this is true in your own case. For a start you have an excellent grasp of how the language *works*—otherwise you wouldn't be able to read this book. In addition, you almost certainly have heard of a number of basic grammatical terms such as 'sentence' and 'verb'. You may not feel entirely confident to explain what they mean, but you have heard of them and will have a general idea of what they mean. (You will know, for example, that it is reasonable to say, 'Every sentence should have at least one verb in it', but crazy to say, 'Every verb must have at least one sentence in it.')

So, very few people start from absolute zero. Nevertheless grammar can *seem* daunting. A major part of the problem is that there's so much of it, and it all seems to be going on at the same time. You begin by trying to understand, for example, what a clause is and before you can turn round, you're being asked to grapple with 'subject', 'finite verb', and 'object'. You start looking at 'subject' and have to contend with 'noun', 'pronoun', and 'noun phrase'. Then, suddenly, you are dragged kicking and screaming into learning about 'headwords' and 'pre-modification'. At least, that's what it feels like.

As far as possible the approach in this part of the book is to take things slowly, one step at a time. You will still find that at times you are being asked to accept grammatical terms that you don't completely understand and that cannot be explained fully until later. This is necessary, because inserting too many quick explanations not only breaks the flow of the main argument, but can also be misleading. If you oversimplify things you sometimes just get them wrong. (If you find taking things on trust becomes too frustrating, you can, of course, always look up the offending terminology in Part B.)

Grammatical levels

One of the things that makes grammar seem complicated is that it operates on a number of different levels, and all are relevant at the same time. Take this sentence, for example:

> *The children watched a television programme while their mother made the tea.*

You could look at any of these features:

- The fact that the sentence breaks down into two sections, each of which is like a mini-sentence on its own:
  The children watched a television programme
  their mother made the tea.

- The idea that within these two bits some of the words seem to stand on their own:
  watched

while others seem to group naturally together:
their mother

- At the other end of the scale you might ask yourself, 'Why does the word "watched" come from "watch" just by adding "-ed", while "make" turns into "made" rather than "maked"?'

These are all different topics from the same sentence; they are different, but clearly interrelated. This is because they work at different levels. In fact grammar has 5 levels:

- **Sentence**
  The children watched television while their mother made the tea.

- **Clause**
  The children watched television

- **Phrase**
  The children

- **Word**
  children

- **Morpheme**
  child – ren

We can show this in a diagram:

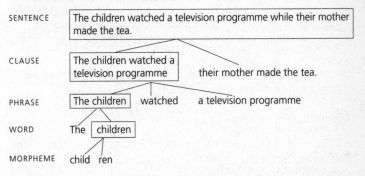

Words

Most people are reasonably happy with the grammatical term 'word'. Words are the building blocks of English. There are hundreds of thousands of them and they fall into two main groups:

■ words that carry the meaning of the sentence

■ words that hold the sentence together

The first group contains words that are sometimes referred to as 'content words', since they have a 'content' of meaning. The content words from the sample sentence above are:

children watched television programme mother made tea

You could look each of these words up in a dictionary and find one or more definitions. For example:

television: *a system for reproducing on a screen visual images transmitted (usu. with sound) by radio signals…* (New Shorter Oxford English Dictionary)

The other group consists of 'structure words', which enable us to construct sentences. They help to join the content words together. In the sample sentence, the structure words are:

The a while their the

If you look these words up in a dictionary you won't find a definition of their meaning, but an explanation of how they are used. For example:

the *(usu. called the* definite article; *in mod. usage also classed as a* determiner) *Designating one or more persons or things already mentioned or known, particularized by context or circumstances, inherently unique, familiar, or otherwise sufficiently identified…* (New Shorter Oxford English Dictionary)

As well as this division into two broad groups, we can place words into a number of word classes. Content words divide into:

■ **nouns**
For example: 'children'

■ **verbs**
For example: 'watched'

■ **adjectives**
For example: 'green'

■ **adverbs**
For example: 'slowly'

Structure words are usually divided into:

- **Pronouns**
  For example: 'they'

- **Conjunctions**
  For example: 'while'

- **Prepositions**
  For example: 'beside'

- **Determiners**
  For example: 'the'

Morphemes

Morphemes are a somewhat more difficult concept. Certain groups of words change their form according to the way in which they are used in sentences. For example:

- Most NOUNS have a singular and plural form:
  child ⟶ children   book ⟶ books
  They can also show possession:
  child ⟶ the child's book

- Most VERBS change their form more extensively:
  walk ⟶ walks ⟶ walking ⟶ walked
  sing ⟶ sings ⟶ singing ⟶ sang ⟶ sung

- Some PRONOUNS change according to whether they are the subject or the object of the clause:
  I ⟶ me   she ⟶ her
  I saw her in the street. She ignored me.

As you can see, most of these involve adding one or more letters to the word: '-s' to make the plural of many nouns, '-ed' to make the past tense of some verbs, and so on. The '-s' and '-ed' are called morphemes. Even when the internal form of the word changes, it is still called a morpheme, so 'sung' is a morpheme of 'sing'.

Phrases

As we move up the scale from simple elements like words, definitions become a little more complex. But it is not too difficult to see the general way in which phrases work in sentences like the following:

> *My long-lost cousin Miriam has been buying a variety of different kinds of fruit.*

It seems natural to break this sentence into three groups of words, or phrases:

My long-lost cousin Miriam	has been buying	a variety of different kinds of fruit

Each of these phrases seems to hang together. If you broke the sentence up in different ways, the groupings would seem artificial. For example:

My long-lost	cousin Miriam has been	buying a variety of	different kinds of fruit.

Each of the first set of phrases could be boiled down to a single word. Admittedly it changes the meaning of the sentence a bit, but it's still recognisable:

My long-lost cousin Miriam	has been buying	a variety of different kinds of fruit
Miriam	bought	fruit.

You cannot do the same with the second arrangement. So phrases can be described as clusters of words that go together and do a particular job in a sentence.

Clauses

The 'Miriam' example shows an important feature of clauses: they are made up of elements that can consist of a single word or a phrase. Each of these elements does a different job in the process of communicating something:

My long-lost cousin Miriam	has been buying	a variety of different kinds of fruit
Miriam	bought	fruit.
this part tells us what the clause is about	**this part gives information about an action**	**this part gives information about the person or thing affected by that action**
SUBJECT	VERB	OBJECT

So clauses are built up of components like subjects, objects, and verbs. At the heart of the clause is the verb.

Sentences

Sentences are notoriously difficult to define. Sometimes it is suggested that a sentence is 'the complete expression of a single thought'. Which sounds all right, until you think of examples like these:

> *Danger!*
> *Damn!*

They are complete expressions of a single thought, but are they sentences? Or look at the following, which is undoubtedly a sentence grammatically:

> *Peter thought for a while about his predicament: he could wait until dawn to see if the others arrived, or he could press on to the top of the ridge, where he hoped there might be a clearer path; but if he did that, who knew what new dangers might confront him?*

It is a sentence, but is it the complete expression of a *single* thought?

It is probably better to think of how the sentence is related to the clause. At its simplest a sentence is the same as a clause: a simple sentence consists of one clause. For example:

My long-lost cousin Miriam	has been buying	a variety of different kinds of fruit
Miriam	bought	fruit
SUBJECT	VERB	OBJECT

More complicated sentences consist of a number of clauses joined together in a number of different ways. The sentence above about Peter contains a total of nine clauses:

1. Peter thought for a while about his predicament

2. he could wait until dawn to see

3. if the others arrived

4. or he could press on to the top of the ridge

5. where he hoped

6. there might be a clearer path

7. but if he did that

8. who knew

9. what new dangers might confront him

Summing up

When we study grammar, we need to be aware that it works at five levels:

- Sentences

- Clauses

- Phrases

- Words

- Morphemes

Whatever aspect of grammar we are studying, any or all of these levels may be relevant. This makes it difficult to focus on just one of them to the exclusion of the others. So in this book we will not work on grammar level by level. Instead we shall try to keep all five in mind at each stage of the investigation.

Chapter 2:
Sentences & Clauses

In this chapter you can read about these topics:

- **Types of clause**
  Declarative
  Interrogative
  Imperative
  Exclamative

- **Clause components**
  Subject
  Verb
  Object

- **Clause patterns**
  Subject + verb
  Subject + verb + object
  Subject + verb + complement

The purpose of the chapter is to provide a brief introduction to how clauses work. This will then be covered in far greater detail in the succeeding chapters. It is only an introduction, so if you find that you cannot grasp it all at once, there's no need to worry. Learning about grammar is like an ascending spiral: each topic has to be revisited several times, and each time you revisit one your understanding grows.

Types of Clause

Most of the time the form of a clause varies according to the communicative purpose it serves, as is illustrated in the following table:

TYPE OF CLAUSE	PURPOSE	EXAMPLE
DECLARATIVE	making statements	*They clapped.*
INTERROGATIVE	asking questions	*Did they clap?*
IMPERATIVE	making commands and requests	*Clap now!*
EXCLAMATIVE	making exclamations	*How they clapped!*

In the table the four types are listed in order of frequency: statements are the most common, followed by questions, and so on. Each type of clause has a typical structure, which is described below.

Declarative

In a declarative sentence the normal word order is:

SUBJECT	VERB	REST OF SENTENCE
They	walked	home.

In longer sentences other words may be inserted in different places:

After the match   they   slowly   walked home.

but the order of subject and verb remains the same.

Interrogative

In an interrogative sentence often part or all of the verb comes before the subject:

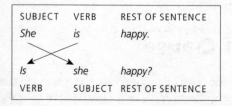

SUBJECT	VERB	REST OF SENTENCE
She	is	happy.
Is	she	happy?
VERB	SUBJECT	REST OF SENTENCE

Sometimes the form of the verb changes in a question, too:

SUBJECT	VERB	REST OF SENTENCE
They	walked	home.

Did	they	walk	home?
VERB	SUBJECT	VERB	REST OF SENTENCE

The chief exception to the change in word order is questions that have 'who' or 'what' as their subject:

> Who said that?
> What caused the damage?

There are three different types of question, categorised according to the kind of answer expected:

1. **Yes/No questions**
   As the name suggests, these expect the answers 'Yes' or 'No'.
   Did they walk home?

2. **Question-word questions**
   These begin with these words:
   who(m), which, what, when, where, why, how

   For example:
   Where did they walk?
   Because of the form of the question words, these questions are sometimes called 'Wh- questions'.

3. **Either/Or questions**
   In these the person addressed is given a choice of two possible answers. For example:
   Did they walk home or go by bus?
   or
   Did they walk home or back to the station?

Imperative

In imperative sentences, the subject is usually omitted, but is understood to be 'you':

> STATEMENT: *They go home.*
> COMMAND: *Go home!*

It is also possible to begin a command with 'You':

> *You stay there!*

Exclamative

These are relatively uncommon and normally begin with a special use of the question words 'what' and 'how'. For example:

> *What a dirty look he gave her!*

As this example shows, exclamations require a radical change of word order from a statement:

STATEMENT | He gave her | a dirty look.

EXCLAMATION | What | a dirty look | he gave her.

Meaning and form

In general we use declarative sentences to make statements, interrogative sentences to ask questions, and so on. This is not, however, always the case. It is, for example, perfectly possible to ask a question using a declarative sentence form. For example:

> *He's going to the cinema this evening?*

In speech, of course, we use a different pattern of tones to indicate that it is a question: a statement ends with a tone that falls at the end, while a sentence that follows a statement pattern but is intended as a question, is spoken with a tone that rises at the end.

You can also give orders using a declarative sentence form:

> *Students are forbidden to walk on the grass.*

You can even give orders using a question pattern, for example the schoolteacher's

> *Will you sit down and be quiet!*

It is an infuriating feature of English grammar that although there are grammatical forms (some call them 'rules) which we normally use to convey particular kinds of meaning, there is often a different way of doing the same thing (which might be said to 'break the rules').

Clause patterns

Since declarative sentences (or statements) are the commonest type, they will form the basis of the analysis that follows. As we have seen, the other types of sentence can be derived from them, following a number of fairly simple rules.

As we saw in the previous chapter, a sentence can consist of just one clause. Such sentences are described as 'simple' sentences. In this chapter we'll focus on very short simple sentences, which will make it much easier to see their structure.

There are seven basic patterns for constructing clauses, but some are much more common than others. The three commonest are introduced in this chapter. This will provide you with enough information to understand Chapters 3 & 4. In Chapter 5, another two patterns are introduced, while the remaining two are covered in Chapter 7. For the sake of completeness all seven are listed, with examples, at the end of this chapter.

Subject

Statement sentences usually begin with a subject. (And if the subject isn't right at the beginning, it should be *near* the beginning.) This makes sense, since the subject normally gives some idea of what the sentence will be about. For example in the sentence *Polonius hid behind a curtain*, we know from the outset that the sentence is going to be about Polonius. In conversation, if someone said, 'Polonius…' our response would be 'What about Polonius?'

The subject of a sentence is usually one of the following:

■ a noun

■ a pronoun

■ a group of words based on a noun, called a noun phrase

Nouns and pronouns are described in greater detail in Chapter 3; noun phrases in Chapter 4.

Predicate

The rest of the sentence in effect answers the question 'What about Polonius?' This part is called the predicate:

SUBJECT	PREDICATE
Polonius	hid behind a curtain.
Polonius	listened.
Polonius	died from a sword thrust.

Verb

The predicate can contain a number of different elements, but in a full sentence, it *must* contain a verb. If we say that the subject generally tells us what the sentence is about, the verb then moves the sentence along by giving information about an action or a state, or by linking the subject to something that comes later on. So, for example, a sentence that begins with the subject 'Hamlet…' can continue:

> *Hamlet hesitated.*
> *Hamlet disappeared.*
> *Hamlet pondered.*

and so on.

Pattern 1: SUBJECT + VERB

This gives us our first basic clause pattern. The minimum that the predicate has to contain is a verb, so a complete sentence can be made by combining a subject and a verb. For brevity this is sometimes written as S+V, or SV:

SUBJECT	VERB
Hamlet	hesitated.

Pattern 2: SUBJECT + VERB + OBJECT

Sometimes the SV pattern is obviously incomplete. For example a sentence with 'Hamlet' as its subject might continue:

> *Hamlet stabbed*

This leaves the listener or reader asking, 'Who did Hamlet stab?' The sentence needs a third element: the object. The object of a sentence is described in two ways:

- It completes the verb, which would otherwise be incomplete.

- It refers to the person, thing or idea affected by the action of the verb.

If you are relatively new to grammar, neither of these definitions helps very much. The first is true, but a bit vague, and the second seems not to apply to a lot of verbs and objects. In the sentence, 'Joseph dreamed a dream' it is difficult to see in what way the dream was affected by Joseph dreaming it. If you are on an object-spotting hunt, it is more helpful to remember that:

- **The object normally comes after the verb in a statement sentence.**

- **It refers to a different person, thing, or idea from the subject.**
  (With the very small exception of objects that are words ending in '-self. In the sentence, 'I cut myself', the subject and object refer to the same person.)

So our second clause pattern is SUBJECT + VERB + OBJECT (S+V+O, or SVO):

SUBJECT	VERB	OBJECT
Hamlet	stabbed	Polonius

The object of a clause can be:

- a noun

- a pronoun

- a noun phrase

Pattern 3: SUBJECT + VERB + COMPLEMENT

So far we have looked at two different kinds of verb:

- verbs that don't need anything after them

- verbs that need an object after them

There is another small group of verbs that work in a different way.

By far the commonest of these is 'be'. If you start a sentence like this:

> *Hamlet was*

it is incomplete, but prompts a different kind of question: 'What was Hamlet?' Possible answers might be:

> *...foolish.*
> *...a king's son.*
> *...solitary.*

and so on. The major difference between these and an object is that they **refer to the same person as the subject**, so the verb is working as a kind of equals sign:

Hamlet	was	solitary.
Hamlet	=	solitary.

The part of the clause that follows the verb is called the subject complement, or more briefly, the complement. The clause pattern is: SUBJECT + VERB + COMPLEMENT (S+V+C or SVC):

SUBJECT	VERB	COMPLEMENT
Hamlet	was	solitary.

A complement can be:

■ a noun

■ a pronoun

■ a noun phrase

■ an adjective

■ a group of words based on an adjective (an adjective phrase)

FACTBOX: Clause patterns

There are seven basic clause patterns in English:

SUBJECT	VERB
Hamlet	hesitated.

SUBJECT	VERB	OBJECT
Hamlet	stabbed	Polonius.

SUBJECT	VERB	COMPLEMENT
Hamlet	was	solitary.

SUBJECT	VERB	INDIRECT OBJECT	DIRECT OBJECT
Hamlet	gave	people	surprises.

SUBJECT	VERB	OBJECT	COMPLEMENT
Hamlet	drove	Ophelia	mad.

SUBJECT	VERB	ADVERBIAL
Hamlet	went	away.

SUBJECT	VERB	OBJECT	ADVERBIAL
Hamlet	put	the sword	down.

Chapter 3:
Nouns & Pronouns

In this chapter you can read about these topics:

- **Nouns**
  Proper nouns
  Common nouns—countable and uncountable

- **Pronouns**
  Different types of pronoun
  Personal pronouns—subjective, objective, possessive
  Reflexive pronouns
  Demonstrative pronouns
  Indefinite pronouns
  Interrogative pronouns
  Relative pronouns

In the previous chapter we saw that each of the following clause components could be, among other things, either a noun or a pronoun:

- subject

- object

- complement

In this chapter we look in more detail at what nouns and pronouns are and how we use them.

Nouns

Many people learn at school that a noun is 'the name of a person, place, thing, or idea'. This definition is quite useful as far as it goes, but it doesn't deal, for example, with the two words in bold in the following example, although they are both nouns:

> *I'd rather go for a **walk** than a **run**.*

As we saw in Chapter 1 such notional definitions are only of limited value in grammar. It is better to define grammatical terms by describing how they work.

FACTBOX: Nouns

Most nouns satisfy all or most of the following tests:

- they can be preceded by *a, an,* or *the*:

  *a **bus**, an **orange**, the **book***

- they have a singular and a plural form:

  *one **bus**, two **buses***

- they can form the headword of a noun phrase (this is explained more fully in the next chapter):

  *the last **bus** for Norwood*

- they can be preceded by an adjective (also described in the next chapter):

  *red **buses**, ripe **oranges***

Nouns fall into a number of different groupings, which can be illustrated by this simple diagram:

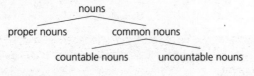

Proper nouns

Proper nouns are a group of words that refer to people, places, or things that are unique. In written English they are spelt with an initial capital letter:

> *Australia   Peter   Parliament*

(You might reasonably object that there is more than one 'Peter' in the world, but within any English sentence when we use the word 'Peter' it refers to a person who is unique in the text.)

Common nouns

All nouns that are not proper nouns are called common nouns. As can be seen from the diagram, they fall into two groups: countable and uncountable.

Countable nouns

Countable nouns refer to people, places, and things which can be counted and so such nouns have a plural form:

> *roses   children   mice*

Most English nouns form their plural by adding 's', but a few, like *mice* and *children* do so in other ways. There are also some words such as *sheep* and *deer* which have the same form for singular and plural. (And words like *fish*, which have two plurals: *fish* and *fishes*.)

Uncountable nouns

There is a smaller group of nouns which refer to things and ideas which cannot be counted. These are generally abstract ideas, like *innocence* and things which we think of in the mass rather than as single or plural objects—like *mud*, or *snow*. Quite a few uncountable nouns, however, can sometimes be used in the plural. For example *butter* is normally uncountable, but we might use it in the plural in a sentence like this:

> *There were several French **butters** at the supermarket today.*

WRITING TIP: Countable and uncountable nouns

There are certain groups of words which can be used before countables and not before uncountables, and vice versa:

WORD(S)	COUNTABLES	COUNTABLES	UNCOUNTABLES
	SINGULAR	PLURAL	
little, less, least	no	no	yes
few, fewer	no	yes	no

continued ▶

WORD(S)	COUNTABLES SINGULAR	COUNTABLES PLURAL	UNCOUNTABLES
much	no	no	yes
many, several	no	yes	no
these	no	yes	no

The only words that are likely to cause problems are 'less' and 'fewer'. We use 'less' with uncountables, but fewer with countables. Many people follow a false pattern:

more mud ⟶ more books
less mud ⟶ less* books

Since books are countable, it should be 'fewer'.

WRITING TIP: Abstract nouns

Nouns are sometimes grouped by meaning into abstract and concrete. Abstract nouns are those which refer to feelings, ideas, and other mental constructs; concrete nouns refer to people, places, and things which can be experienced using the five senses:

ABSTRACT	CONCRETE
happiness	car
success	keyboard
truth	sand
beauty	tree

It is sometimes argued that, if possible, you should avoid using too many abstract nouns. While it is true that a text stuffed with abstracts can be longwinded and even difficult to read, the examples quoted show that the list of abstract nouns contains many words which are frequently used in ordinary speech. Avoiding them would be pointless and counter-productive.

> ### FACTBOX: Verbal noun
>
> A verbal noun, or 'gerund' is the -ing form of the verb used as a noun:
>
> > **Smoking** *is forbidden.*
> > *I love* **eating** *ice cream.*
>
> Because a verbal noun is partly a noun and partly a verb, it can cause problems when preceded by a noun or pronoun. For example, is it:
>
> > *She does not like* **my** *smoking in the house.*
> > *She does not like* **Peter's** *smoking in the house.*
>
> or
>
> > *She does not like* **me** *smoking in the house.*
> > *She does not like* **Peter** *smoking in the house.*
>
> The former, using the genitive, is accepted by traditionalists but appears to be on the way out. It is advisable to stick to this usage, however, in formal writing and speech, when referring to people.

Pronouns

As we have seen, the subject of a sentence can be a pronoun. The name 'pronoun' indicates that these words stand in for ('pro') something else. Sometimes pronouns stand in for nouns:

> *David had a strange experience yesterday.* **He** *was coming home from work at the normal time…*

They can also stand in for other words, or groups of words; they can even stand in more generally for ideas and information already mentioned. This short paragraph illustrates some of them. The pronouns are printed in bold.

> *George was one of the old school.* **He** *always remained calm, however great the provocation.* **This** *was just as well on the occasion* **I** *last met* **him, which** *was on the first Monday of May 1992.* **It** *happened to be raining…*

1. The uses of *he* and *him* are examples of a pronoun replacing a noun, 'George'. Similarly *I* is used to refer to the writer.

2. *This* refers to a general idea: the fact that George always remained calm.

3. *Which* refers to a noun phrase, 'the occasion I last met him'.

4. *It* doesn't refer back to anything at all. It is called a 'dummy subject'—it is a useful way of constructing that kind of sentence.

WRITING TIP

It + passive
A common usage is to begin a sentence with it, followed by a passive. For example:

> *It is felt that your actions were inappropriate.*

Here the writer is trying to avoid responsibility, by refusing to use the active and give the verb a subject. (Compare: 'I think you behaved badly.') Such usage is mealy-mouthed.
On the other hand, the construction may be quite useful:

> *It is believed that production figures for the third quarter are well down.*

The writer may well not have a clear idea of exactly whose opinion is being quoted, although it is quite clear that the belief is widespread. In such a case the use of *It* + passive is useful.

WRITING TIP

Most pronouns refer back to a word, a phrase, or an idea that has already been mentioned. It is essential to make sure that it is clear to the reader to what each pronoun refers. Sometimes, when, for example, the text mentions more than one person or thing, the use of pronouns can be confusing:

> *George and Mr Malahyde met at the appointed time. He greeted him enthusiastically but his reply was not encouraging.*

continued ▶

Who greeted whom? And whose reply was not encouraging?
If there is any doubt, repeat the word, phrase or idea rather than
using a pronoun:

> *George and Mr Malahyde met at the appointed time. George*
> *greeted him enthusiastically but Malahyde's reply was not*
> *encouraging.*

Different types of pronoun

Pronouns have many uses and so it is not surprising that there are
several different groups, which are formed and used in different
ways. They are listed in the box below.

FACTBOX: Pronouns

Pronouns stand in for nouns, other pronouns, groups of words or,
more generally, for ideas and information already mentioned. They
commonly refer back to these, but can sometimes also refer forwards
in a text. There are these types of pronoun:

Personal	I/me, we/us, you, he/him, she/her, it, they/them
Possessive	mine, ours, yours, his, hers, its, theirs
Reflexive	myself, ourselves, yourself, yourselves, himself, herself, itself, themselves
Demonstrative	this, that, these, those
Indefinite	some, someone, somebody, something any, anyone, anybody, anything none, no one, nobody, nothing everyone, everybody, everything, all either, neither, both, each
Interrogative	who, whom, whose, what, which
Relative	who, whom, whose, which, that

Personal pronouns

Personal pronouns refer back to nouns which have already been used in a text:

> **David** had a strange experience yesterday. **He** was coming home from work at the normal time…

They are also sometimes used to refer forwards:

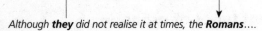

> Although **they** did not realise it at times, the **Romans**….

In the previous two examples personal pronouns have been used to refer to people, but this is not why they are called 'personal'; they can also be used to refer to animals and indeed anything else that can be represented by a noun in a sentence:

> The **geese** were tired after their long journey from Africa, but it was not until **they** reached the Severn Estuary…
>
> **Happiness** is not something you can buy. **It** is something only the fortunate are granted.

Subjective, Objective, Possessive

Personal pronouns come in three forms:

SUBJECTIVE	OBJECTIVE	POSSESSIVE
I	me	mine
we	us	ours
you	you	yours
she	her	hers
he	him	his
it	it	its
they	them	theirs

The **SUBJECTIVE** form is used for the subject of the sentence, and, in formal English, after the verb 'to be':

> *'Who is that at the door?' – 'It is **I**.'*

In colloquial English, however, people more often say, 'It's **me**.'

The **OBJECTIVE** form is used for the object of the sentence (see Chapter 3):

> *That dog bit me.*

and after prepositions:

> *I want you to give it to **her**.*

The **POSSESSIVE** form, as its name expresses, shows that something belongs to a person or thing referred to:

> *Mary told Ewan that the book was **hers**.*
> *I apologise: the mistake was **mine**.*

But what about *my, our* and *her*?

There is another group of words used to show possession:

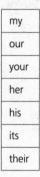

| my |
| our |
| your |
| her |
| his |
| its |
| their |

Examples

> *That is **my** book. I tell you it's **mine!***
> *Shona says that's **her** house. It's the one next door to **yours**.*

As you can see, words from this second group (*my, our*, etc) always come before a noun. Words from the first group (*mine, our*, etc) stand alone.

my, our, your, his, her, their are sometimes described as 'possessive pronouns'. There are two problems with doing this:

1. It is confusing. As we have just seen, 'mine', 'ours' etc have already occupied this slot. To give another set of words the same name doesn't help.

2. Pronouns are words that can stand on their own—in place of another word, expression, or idea. These words cannot stand on their own. They must always be followed by a noun: 'my pen', 'your pullover', and so on.

Some writers call them 'possessive adjectives'—they show possession and come before a noun. But they aren't much like adjectives, because you can't do to them the things you can do to adjectives. You only have to compare 'my' and 'fast' in these sentences to see the difference:

That's a very fast car.	That's a very my car.*
That car is fast.	That car is my.*

The best way to think of these words is as *possessive determiners*. This means that they behave more like 'a' and 'the':

That's a new car.	That's my new car.

There is more about determiners in the next chapter, on pages 33–4.

Reflexive pronouns

myself	ourselves
yourself	yourselves
herself	themselves
himself	
itself	

Reflexive pronouns are used in sentences like these:

> He cut **himself** with a knife.
> Mary gave **herself** a pat on the back.

In these sentences the use of a reflexive pronoun makes it clear that the subject and the object of the sentence refer to the same person. To see why this is necessary, you only need to remove '-self'. For example:

> He cut **him** with a knife.

Now it appears that there are two different people involved: 'He' and the person 'he' cut.

Another use for reflexive pronouns is for emphasis. This sentence:

> I promised to do it **myself**.

is much stronger than:

> I promised to do it.

Demonstrative pronouns

this	these
that	those

Most of the time the use of these is fairly straightforward: we use 'this' and 'these' to refer to people or things near at hand and 'that' and 'those' to refer to things further away.

WRITING TIP

Demonstratives are very useful to show how parts of a text link together. We can use them to refer back to a sentence or idea that has already been dealt with:

> The Russian invasion of Chechnya was not opposed by the West. **This** was largely because the West had had its own way over the peacekeeping mission to Kosovo.

It is important to make sure that the reference is clear. In the following sentence, for example, that is not the case:

> The Russian invasion of Chechnya was not opposed by the West, or even seriously discussed in the United Nations Security Council. **This** was largely because the West had had its own way over the peacekeeping mission to Kosovo.

continued ▶

In the first sentence of that example there are two statements: 'The Russian invasion of Chechnya was not opposed by the West' and 'The Russian invasion of Chechnya…(was not)…even seriously discussed in the United Nations Security Council.' The 'This' which starts the next sentence could refer to either of these—or, indeed, both of them. So the text needs to be recast:

> The Russian invasion of Chechnya was not opposed by the West, or even seriously discussed in the United Nations Security Council. **Both these things** were largely because the West had had its own way over the peacekeeping mission to Kosovo.

Indefinite pronouns

some	someone	somebody	something		
any	anyone	anybody	anything	either	
none	no one	nobody	nothing	neither	
all	everyone	everybody	everything	both	each

As you can see from the list, these refer to people or things in a way that ranges from general (*all*) to vague (*someone*). We use them when we want to make general statements and do not wish to be pinned down:

> **Someone** had blundered.
> Has **anybody** seen my pen?

WRITING TIP: *none is* or *none are*?

Some traditionalists say that the pronoun *none* should always be followed by a singular verb: *none is* is always right and *none are* is always wrong. They argue that *none* comes from *no one* and so is always singular. This is mistaken. If you refer to the Oxford English Dictionary, you will find no support for this view. It says that the word

continued ▶

means *not any (one) of a number of persons or things…no one…no persons…* It comments that using it to mean *no persons* is now commoner than using it to mean *no one*. If you wish to make it clear that there was only one individual involved, then you have to say *no one*.

Recent research suggests that *none are* is normal in conversation while *none is* occurs more commonly in written English.

In general, *none* is best followed by the form of the verb which makes better sense, as in the following examples:

> *Of all the people I met in Brentwood, none **is** more influential than Fran Waters.*
>
> *None of the other people I met **have** half her charm.*

Interrogative pronouns

who	whom	whose	which	what

As the name indicates, these are used in questions:

> *Who has taken my umbrella?*
> *Whose fault is it?*
> *What are you doing?*

Relative pronouns

Relative pronouns are used to form relative clauses, which are described in detail in the next chapter, on pages 43–8.

Chapter 4:
Noun phrases

In this chapter you can read about these topics:

- **Noun phrases**
  headword
  determiners
  modifiers

- **Adjectives**
  qualitative adjectives
  classifying adjectives

- **Prepositional phrases and prepositions**

- **Relative clauses**
  what they do
  types of relative clause
  defining and non-defining relative clauses

Noun phrases

As we saw in the previous chapter, a noun can stand alone as the subject, object, or complement of a clause or simple sentence. Much more often, however, a noun forms the centre of a larger group of words: a noun phrase. In the following sentence, the subject is a noun:

> **Children** are playing in the park.

We can build this up into a noun phrase like this:

> **The children** are playing in the park.
> **The naughty children** are playing in the park.
> **The naughty children from next door** are playing in the park.
> **The naughty children who live next door** are playing in the park.

However long this noun phrase becomes, it is always based on the same noun, *children*. This is called the **headword** of the phrase. A noun phrase can always be reduced to a single headword:

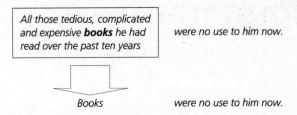

| All those tedious, complicated and expensive **books** he had read over the past ten years | *were no use to him now.* |

Books   *were no use to him now.*

A noun phrase is built up by adding words **before** and **after** the headword:

	BEFORE	HEADWORD	AFTER
1	the	children	
2	the naughty	children	
3	the naughty	children	from next door
4	the naughty	children	who come from next door

Words that come before the headword

Determiners

If you think about it, a lot of nouns are fairly helpless on their own. Some can stand on their own:

> *Helen arrived today.* (PROPER NOUN)
> *Success is like a drug.* (UNCOUNTABLE NOUN)
> *Computers are stupid.* (PLURAL NOUN)

Other nouns need something to support them. The following 'sentence' is incomplete, because the noun which starts it cannot stand alone:

> *Book is boring*

We need to add a word before the noun. For example: *this, the, my* or even *any*. Words like this are called **determiners**.

Modifiers

While determiners help to give the noun more definition, modifiers provide more information. They can come before the noun, in which case they are called **premodifiers**; or they can come after it, in which case they are **postmodifiers**.

Premodifiers

The commonest way of premodifying a noun is to add one or more adjectives:

> The **long low red** car swept up the drive.

Other premodifiers include nouns:

> The **England** team left for Australia yesterday.

the -*ing* form of verbs:

> The **distressing** news reached us yesterday.

and the *-ed* form of verbs:

> *Perched on the garden wall there was a* ***broken*** *milk bottle.*

Postmodifiers

The two commonest types of postmodifier are:

1. a prepositional phrase

> *The last person* ***in my thoughts*** *was Rosie.*

2. a relative clause

> *The last person* ***I was expecting to see*** *was Rosie.*

The remainder of this chapter concentrates on:

- ADJECTIVES (pp 36–40)

- PREPOSITIONAL PHRASES (pp 40–3)

- RELATIVE CLAUSES (pp 43–8)

WRITING TIP: Noun phrases

When we are writing, of course, we don't have to think consciously about how noun phrases are constructed. But knowing a little about this can be useful when we encounter problems.

- **Beware of noun phrases that are too long**
  When a writer is trying to be precise it is easy to extend a noun phrase to the point where the reader gets lost:

  > ***The strangely appealing but frequently disconcerting people of this tiny island stuck halfway between Tasmania and Antarctica, far from shipping lanes and remote from so-called civilisation*** *have finally agreed to build an airstrip.*

  Here the writer has tried to cram a lot of information about the local people into an unsuitable place. The solution is to untangle the sentence and start again. You do this by working out the headword of the noun phrase and then deciding how much of the information wrapped round it is really necessary for the sentence

  continued ▶

---

and how much can be put into one or two other sentences. The headword is *people* and the basic sentence is:

> **The people** have finally agreed to build an airstrip.

This doesn't make much sense on its own, so we need to add some of the detail in the original sentence:

> **The people of this tiny island** have finally decided to build an airstrip.

The remaining information can then be conveyed in additional sentences:

> *Their island is stuck halfway between Tasmania and Antarctica, far from shipping lanes and remote from so-called civilisation. Its inhabitants are strangely appealing but frequently disconcerting.*

■ **Make sure that the verb agrees with the subject**
When the subject of a noun phrase is quite long, it is easy to lose track and fail to make the verb agree:

> *Several people who were at the meeting, including my old friend Simon Darnley **has** been in touch with me today by phone.*

In this sentence the verb has been made to agree with the part of the subject nearest to it: *Simon Darnley*. The key is to locate the headword of the noun phrase (in this case, *people*) and make the verb agree with that: *people…**have**…*

Adjectives

At school I learned that adjectives were 'describing words'. For school purposes this is a useful definition; it covers a lot of strong and useful adjectives such as *red, fast, horrible,* and *delicious.* But it doesn't give us a lot of information about how to identify adjectives or about how they can be used. For this we need a formal, or grammatical definition.

FACTBOX: Adjectives

Attributive

Adjectives can be used to modify a noun. They help to give the noun definition by providing more information. They are usually placed before the noun:

A **sweet yellow** fruit appeared on my plate.

They are sometimes placed after the noun:

The heir **apparent** spoke next.

When adjectives are used to modify a noun they are described as **attributive**.

Predicative

Adjectives can also be used after verbs like 'be', as the complement of the clause. They provide more information about the subject:

That view is **extraordinary**.

The answer is **obvious**.

When adjectives are used in this way, they are called 'predicative'. Most adjectives can be used in either way, but a few are limited to one use. Examples are *alone* and *sole*. You cannot talk about 'an alone man', or say, 'That purpose is sole'.

Adjectives can also be grouped into **qualitative** and **classifying**.

Qualitative adjectives

Some adjectives tell us about the qualities of a person, thing, or idea. For example:

easy   fast   minuscule   practical

Adjectives of this type can be **graded**: we can add to them in various ways to state more precisely how much of the quality we wish to add to the noun:

an **easy** decision

a **fairly easy** decision

an **extremely easy** decision

and so on.

We can also compare two or more people, things, or ideas:

*The decision was **easier** than the previous one.*
*It was the **easiest** decision of my life.*

So every qualitative adjective has three forms:

ABSOLUTE	COMPARATIVE	SUPERLATIVE
fast	faster	fastest
easy	easier	easiest
rapid	more rapid	most rapid
extraordinary	more extraordinary	most extraordinary

As can be seen from the table, words of more than two syllables don't add -*er* and -*est*, but are preceded by *more* and *most*. Two syllable words vary: some add -*er* and -*est* and some use *more* and *most*. Confusingly, some, like *stupid* can do either.

WRITING TIP: Comparing things

It is correct Standard English to use the comparative when only two items are involved and reserve the superlative for three or more. So the following sentence is incorrect:

My sister is the oldest of the two of us.

It should be 'older'. Increasingly, however, even educated speakers seem to see nothing wrong with 'oldest' in sentences like that.

Classifying adjectives

Another group of adjectives places items into categories. For example:

annual   nuclear   actual

By contrast with qualitative adjectives, classifying adjectives cannot normally be graded. You cannot, for example, have a 'rather annual' event—either it is annual or it isn't. Nor could you describe a weapon as 'fairly nuclear'. As always, however, there are grey areas; people use language creatively and 'break the rules'.

Conventionally 'pregnant' is a classifying adjective, so it should be 'wrong' to describe a woman as 'slightly pregnant'. But you will hear statements such as, 'She was looking very pregnant when I saw her.' The meaning of pregnant has expanded from the classifying 'with child' to 'large with child', which can sometimes be qualitative rather than classifying.

WRITING TIP: *quite*

The adverb 'quite' has a range of uses of which a very common one is as a MODIFIER used before an adjective or adverb:

> *That is quite impossible.*
> *She moved forward quite slowly.*

It has two meanings, however:

- **'completely'**
  quite impossible

- **'fairly'**
  quite slowly

If 'quite' modifies an adjective or adverb that can be graded, the second meaning is usually intended, as in the example above. Otherwise it is the first. This is not always true, however, and confusion can arise:

> *Their garden is quite beautiful.*

Does the speaker mean 'fairly' or 'completely' here? (Or is the statement deliberately ambiguous?)

WRITING TIP: *unique*

The Oxford English Dictionary defines 'unique' as meaning 'of which there is only one'. As a result, some people get very irritated when it is graded, as in this phrase from *Country Life* in 1939:

> *Almost the most unique residential site along the South Coast...*

continued ▶

Others argue that 'unique' as well as meaning 'the only one of its kind' can also mean 'unusual' or 'remarkable'—in which case it can be graded. Indeed, even if you take the stricter view, you must still allow 'unique' to be preceded by 'almost':

> *The site was almost unique on the South Coast.*

since this simply means 'almost the only one of its kind', which is clearly allowable. As with many things in language use, it is a matter of judgement. If you want to be safe, reserve 'unique' to mean 'the only one of its kind' and never grade it. If you want a similar meaning, with grading, then use an adjective such as 'rare'.

Prepositional phrases

Adjectives are an obvious way of giving a noun more definition. We can extend that precision by adding more and more adjectives to the string of premodifiers. But there is another way, and that is by adding words after the headword. For example:

> *a new product* **with many exciting features**
> *that family* **down the road**

Both the phrases in bold begin with a preposition and are described as prepositional phrases.

Prepositions

Prepositions are a small group of small words. They are placed (**position**ed) before (**pre**) one of the following:

- a noun
  with *marbles*

- a pronoun
  to *me*

- the -ing form of the verb
  for *walking*

- a noun phrase
  down *a long dusty road*

FACTBOX: Prepositions

Most prepositions, but by no means all, are single words, usually quite short. The commonest are:

about	above	across	after	against	along
among	around	as	at	before	behind
below	beneath	beside	between	beyond	but
by	despite	during	except	for	from
in	inside	into	less	like	near
of	off	on	onto*	over	past
round	since	through	throughout	till	to
towards	under	underneath	until	up	upon
with	within	without			

It is also possible to have prepositions that consist of two, three, or even four words. For example:

along with	apart from	as well as	away from
because of	close to	except for	in front of
in spite of	in the face of	instead of	next to
on to*	on top of	out of	owing to
up to			

* Both 'on to' and 'onto' appear in the tables, because both are used. 'Onto' is a compound preposition, like 'into', but it hasn't moved so far along the road of acceptance, so while both 'on to' and 'onto' are possible, some writers prefer the two-word version.

Structure of prepositional phrases

Prepositions frequently precede noun phrases, but since noun phrases can themselves contain preposition phrases, the structure can become quite complicated. For example:

a book about problems in certain countries of SE Asia

This is a noun phrase which contains two more noun phrases each of which has a noun phrase embedded in it, so that altogether we are looking at four noun phrases:

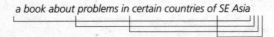

This feature of the relationship between noun phrases and prepositional phrases can cause problems for writers and readers. When you are writing, for example, you may find that a noun phrase gets out of control, so that you are no longer sure whether it is singular or plural. In the example above there are four headwords ('book', 'problems', 'countries', 'Asia'). Of these two are singular and two are plural. But only one is the headword of the whole noun phrase—'book'—and that is the noun with which the verb should agree.

WRITING TIP: Prepositions at the end of sentences

There are still people who say that you should never end a sentence with a preposition. They argue that since the term 'preposition' describes a word that is positioned **before** ('pre-') another word it is wrong to place it at the end of a sentence, where it cannot come before anything. In fact it is sometimes necessary to put a preposition at the end, since there is no other way of constructing the sentence.

The alternative didn't bear thinking about.

Sometimes it is possible to reword a sentence to avoid putting a preposition at the end. This sentence:

This is the book you asked for.

can be recast as:

This is the book for which you asked.

The alternative version, however, is much more formal, and many would find it a little pompous. In fact, it is only in academic texts that writers try to avoid placing a preposition at the end of a sentence. In most other writing, this is a 'rule' that you can happily ignore.

FACTBOX: Prepositional phrases

Prepositional phrases consist of a preposition, followed by:

■ a noun

■ a pronoun

■ the -ing form of the verb

■ a noun phrase

Prepositional phrases are used as a postmodifier in a noun phrase (they come after the headword). They are also used as adverbials and this is described in Chapter 8, page 89.

Relative clauses

Relative clauses do a similar job to adjectives:

> She was wearing a **red striped** scarf. (adjectives)
> She was wearing a scarf **that had red stripes on it**. (relative clause)

In their fullest form, relative clauses are like mini-sentences. You can remove them from the sentence they are in and with very few changes turn them into sentences in their own right:

ORIGINAL	BECOMES
She was wearing a scarf **that had red stripes on it**.	She was wearing a scarf. **It had red stripes on it**.
The man **you met yesterday** is my uncle.	**You met a man yesterday**. He is my uncle.

Relative pronouns

Relative clauses are introduced by **relative pronouns**:

who	which	that	when
whom			where
whose			why

Most of these can also have *ever* after them:

whoever	whichever	whenever
whomever		wherever

There are also *whosoever* and *whomsoever*. Of all these relative pronouns by far the commonest are: *who, which,* and *that*. It is also fairly common to introduce a relative clause with no pronoun at all (the 'zero relative'). All these are possible:

> *This is the man whom I met yesterday.*
> *This is the man that I met yesterday.*
> *This is the man I met yesterday.*

The relative clauses we have looked at so far contain a **finite verb**. This is explained more fully on pages 52–3. All we need to know at this point is that any verb has these forms:

FINITE	*take, takes, took*
INFINITIVE OR 'TO FORM'	*to take*
PRESENT PARTICIPLE OR '-ING FORM'	*taking*
PAST PARTICIPLE OR '-ED' FORM	*taken*

Each of these forms can be used to postmodify a noun:

FINITE	*She is the person **who took** over the **top job**.*
INFINITIVE, OR 'TO-FORM'	*These are the books **to take** to Denis.*
PRESENT PARTICIPLE OR '-ING FORM'	*She is the person **taking** the **decisions**.*
PAST PARTICIPLE, OR '-ED' FORM	*This is a photograph **taken** yesterday.*

Only the finite form can easily be turned into a separate sentence, as shown above. The other forms require the addition of more words:

ORIGINAL	BECOMES
*These are the books **to take** to Denis.*	*These are the books. **You have to take them to Denis.***
*She is the person **taking the decisions**.*	*She is the person. **She is taking the decisions.***

*This is a photograph **taken**   This is a photograph. **It was taken**
yesterday.   **yesterday**.*

Defining and non-defining relative clauses

We have seen that a relative clause modifies the noun which lies at
the centre of the noun phrase: it adds information. Sometimes that
information is essential. Without it, the noun phrase no longer
makes much sense because the noun headword is not sufficiently
defined:

> *The book I finished yesterday is absolutely gripping.*

> *The book ~~I finished yesterday~~ is absolutely gripping.*

> *The book is absolutely gripping.*

To say simply 'The book is absolutely gripping' is not much use
since it is not clear which book is referred to. Such relative clauses
are described as **defining relative clauses**, since they help define
the noun which they modify.

Non-defining relative clauses, on the other hand, provide
additional information which does not define the noun. In the
following sentence, it is quite clear to whom the noun 'uncle'
refers; sufficient definition is provided by the possessive
determiner 'my':

> *My uncle is staying with us for a few days.*

The implication is that either the speaker only has one uncle, or, if
there is more than one, that we don't need to know which one is
being referred to. So if we add a relative clause it is only for the
purpose of providing additional, non-essential, information:

> *My uncle, who lives in Bradford, is staying with us for a few days.*

Such **non-defining relative clauses** are usually enclosed between
commas (or, sometimes, dashes or brackets).

To check whether a relative clause is defining or non-defining,
try removing it from the sentence. If it is still clear to whom or to
what the noun refers, then the clause is non-defining. Otherwise it
is defining.

WRITING TIP: Punctuating relative clauses

Defining relative clauses should not be marked off by commas; non-defining relative clauses should be enclosed in commas, brackets, or dashes.

Sometimes writers enclose defining relative clauses between commas. This can be confusing, especially for readers who assume that any relative clause between commas is non-defining:

> There will be a farewell party for Miriam on 15th June and all Directors, who are free then, will be most welcome.

Taken literally, this sentence implies that all Directors are free on 15th June, which is not presumably what was intended.

WRITING TIP: *who* or *whom*?

Relative clauses are introduced by the **relative pronouns** *who, whom, whose, which,* and *that.* These can cause some problems, particularly the choice of *who* or *whom.* The traditional rules are these:

1. **Use *who* as the subject of the verb**. *My uncle, **who** comes from Bradford, is staying with us for a few days.* **But see 'Wrong use of *whom*' below**.

2. **Use *whom* as the object of the verb**. *The teacher **whom** I met last week is moving to a new school.* (There is more about objects on pp 15–16.)

3. **Use *whom* after prepositions**. *The official **to whom** I handed my passport looked very suspicious.* (There is more about prepositions and prepositional phrases on pp 40–3.)

Increasingly, however, *who* is replacing *whom* in spoken English:

1. *My uncle, **who** comes from Bradford, is staying with us for a few days.*

2. *The teacher **who** I met last week is moving to a new school.*

3. *The official **who** I handed my passport **to** looked very suspicious.*

continued ▶

On the other hand, most people would still find it strange to hear, *The official **to who** I handed my passport looked very suspicious*.

So it is probably acceptable to use *who* as an object in conversation and in informal writing. But *whom* should still be used as an object in formal writing. *Whom* should always be used immediately after a preposition.

Finally, it is worth pointing out that often we use no relative pronoun at all (the 'zero relative') in preference to *whom*:

> *The teacher I met last week is moving to a new school.*
> *The official I handed my passport to looked very suspicious*.

One way or another, the days of *whom* are probably numbered.

Wrong use of whom

Sometimes those who are afraid of using 'who' when they should use 'whom' over-correct themselves and produce sentences such as:

> *The man **whom** we believe is guilty has escaped from custody.*

Here the relative pronoun is the subject of the verb 'is' and so it should be 'who', not 'whom'.

WRITING TIP: *that* or *which*?

The choice between 'that' and 'which' to introduce relative clauses can sometimes cause problems, which are not helped by some so-called 'grammar checkers'. This is partly a question of custom, and the following table sets out the main points:

Use	that	which
To refer to living creatures	quite common (along with 'who')	almost never
To introduce defining relative clauses	very common	less common
To introduce non-defining relative clauses	almost never	nearly always for inanimate nouns

continued ▶

Use	*that*	*which*
Formal or academic writing	less common	more common
Informal or colloquial writing	more common	less common

When you wish to use a preposition, you have a choice:

> *I knew nothing about the city to which I was going.*
> *I knew nothing about the city that I was going to.*
> *I knew nothing about the city I was going to.*

These are in descending order of formality.

Chapter 5:
Verbs

In this chapter you can read about these topics:

- **Two meanings for 'verb'**
- **What is a sentence verb?**
- **The parts of a verb**
  stem, infinitive, present and past tenses, present and past participles
  regular and irregular verbs
  finite verb forms
- **Classifying verbs**
  transitive, intransitive, and linking
  main and auxiliary
  primary verbs
  modal auxiliaries

One of the problems people often have with the grammatical term 'verb' is that it is used in two different ways:

- It describes a class of words in the same way as 'noun', 'adjective', and 'preposition' do.

- It describes a part of a clause, in the same way as 'subject' and 'object' do.

This chapter deals with both uses, but it is important to remember that they are not the same. We shall begin with the verb as part of a clause.

Definition

If the subject often tells us what the sentence is going to be about, the job of the verb is to develop the subject in some way. In a statement sentence the verb generally comes after the subject:

SUBJECT	VERB	REST OF SENTENCE
He	*ran*	*away.*

It may be a single word, or a group of words:

> *He **ran** away.*
> *He **had been running** for several minutes.*
> *He **should have been visiting** his aunt.*

Verbs are used:

- to express an action
  *She **escaped**.*

- to express a state
  *She **slept**.*

- to link the subject with a later part of the sentence
  *She **was** happy.*

The verb phrase

The verb in a clause is sometimes called the verb phrase. This applies whether it consists of one word or several. If a sentence contains only one clause, then it contains one verb phrase. If it contains more than one clause then there is one verb phrase per clause:

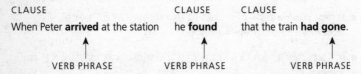

CLAUSE	CLAUSE	CLAUSE
When Peter **arrived** at the station	he **found**	that the train **had gone**.
↑	↑	↑
VERB PHRASE	VERB PHRASE	VERB PHRASE

Parts of a verb

If a word has more than one form, we say that it inflects. For example, nouns inflect to show whether they are singular or plural: *one book, two books*. English does not have many inflections and most of them affect verbs. English verbs have the five forms illustrated in this set of sentences:

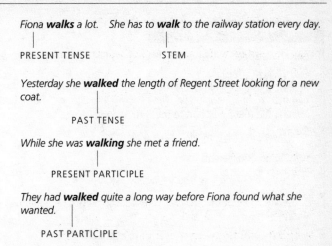

*Fiona **walks** a lot.   She has to **walk** to the railway station every day.*

PRESENT TENSE   STEM

*Yesterday she **walked** the length of Regent Street looking for a new coat.*

PAST TENSE

*While she was **walking** she met a friend.*

PRESENT PARTICIPLE

*They had **walked** quite a long way before Fiona found what she wanted.*

PAST PARTICIPLE

In a regular verb, all these forms are based on the verb stem 'walk'; you simply add the endings '-ing', '-ed' and '-s' to create the other verb forms. Here are the parts of the verb presented as a table:

FACTBOX: Forms of the verb			
STEM	walk	swim	be
PRESENT TENSE	walk/walks	swim/swims	am/is/are
PRESENT PARTICIPLE	walking	swimming	being
PAST TENSE	walked	swam	was/were
PAST PARTICIPLE	walked	swum	been

Many verbs follow the pattern of 'walk'. These verbs are 'regular'. Other verbs, like 'go' depart from the pattern. So, for example, instead of saying 'goed' for the past tense, we say 'went'. These verbs are 'irregular'. There are relatively few irregular verbs, but they include many of the commonest verbs. As can be seen from the table, the verb 'be' is very irregular.

WRITING TIP: 'Swang'?

Even native speakers who have been using English all their lives can find irregular verbs confusing. They follow a variety of different rules and sometimes we apply the rule for one verb to another. It is quite common to hear people say, 'They **swang** into action.' They have applied the rule for 'swim' to the verb 'swing':

> swim: I swim, I swam, I have swum

But 'swing' is different:

> swing: I swing, I swung, I have swung

These are some of the irregular verbs that some people either get wrong or have to think about:

STEM ('swim')	PAST TENSE ('I swam')	PAST PARTICIPLE ('I have swum')
burst	burst	burst
cast	cast	cast
drive	drove	driven
forbid	forbade	forbidden
forsake	forsook	forsaken
freeze	froze	frozen
lay	laid	laid
lead	led	led
ride	rode	ridden
rise	rose	risen
saw	sawed	sawn
shake	shook	shaken
slay	slew	slain
stride	strode	stridden
strive	strove	striven
swing	swung	swung
thrust	thrust	thrust

Finite verb forms

Only two of the forms in the table on page 51 can be used on their own as the verb of a clause. These are the present tense and past tense forms. The present tense has more than one form, because it has to agree with the subject in number and person. What this means and how it works are shown in the table on page 53:

FACTBOX: Number and person

	SINGULAR	PLURAL
1ST PERSON	I walk	we walk
2ND PERSON	you walk (thou walkest)	you walk
3RD PERSON	he/she/it walks	they walk

The verb 'be' shows far more variation:

	SINGULAR	PLURAL
1ST PERSON	I am	we are
2ND PERSON	you are (thou art)	you are
3RD PERSON	he/she/it is	they are

The past and present tense forms are described as 'finite', meaning that they are complete and can stand on their own. Other non-finite forms need the help of other verb words to form a verb phrase. For example:

STEM	*walk*	We **could** walk home.
PRESENT PARTICIPLE	*walking*	We **are** walking home.
PAST PARTICIPLE	*walked*	We **have** walked home.

WRITING TIP: Agreement

It is fairly easy to fail to make the subject and verb agree, especially if the subject is an extended noun phrase. If this consists of a list joined by 'and' the verb should be plural, but sometimes writers make the verb agree with the final element of the list:

Marcus, Julia, Harold, and I am planning a trip to Huddersfield. (Should be 'are'.)

If the subject is singular but contains within it some kind of reference to a plural, the reverse mistake can be made:

Marcus Wade, a close friend of Julia and Harold, are planning a trip to Huddersfield. (Should be 'is'.)

Classifying verbs

As we have seen, only the present and past tense forms can be used on their own as the verb phrase in a clause. All the other forms need the help of another verb word to form the verb phrase in a sentence. The verbs that do this 'helping' job are called 'auxiliary verbs'. Other verbs are called 'main verbs'.

Main verbs

Main verbs can be divided, according to the way in which they work in the sentence. They can be:

- transitive
- intransitive
- linking

Transitive and intransitive verbs

Some sentences are mainly about the subject: they give us information about the persons, things, or ideas referred to in the subject, but do not refer to any other persons, things, or ideas. Sentences like these consist either of just a subject and verb, or subject, verb, and adverbial. For example:

> *The building collapsed.*   (SUBJECT + VERB)
> *The car disappeared from view.*   (SUBJECT + VERB + ADVERBIAL)

Verbs that can be used in sentences like this are described as **intransitive**. Examples of intransitive verbs are:

arrive	depart	die	disappear
exist	fall	happen	occur
recede	rise	surrender	vanish

There is more information about certain types of intransitive verb in Chapter 8 on adverbials.

Other sentences refer both to the subject and to some other person, thing, or idea. Sentences like these follow the pattern:

SUBJECT + VERB + OBJECT

For example:

> *Vandals have damaged the trees in the park.*
> *I blame the schools.*

Verbs like *damage* and *blame* which can be used in sentences like these are described as transitive verbs. Examples of transitive verbs are:

admire	avoid	buy	complete	cover	create
cut	damage	demand	destroy	discover	enjoy
expect	find	get	give	hit	keep
like	love	make	mean	need	own
prefer	produce	raise	receive	remove	risk
seek	take	use	want	wear	

Verbs that are both transitive and intransitive

Some verbs can be either. For example the verb 'run' can be used with or without an object:

> *They were running.*
> *Mrs Hayes ran a shop.*

Active and passive

Transitive verbs can be used in two different ways or 'voices', active and passive:

> ACTIVE: *Your dog **bit** me.*
> PASSIVE: *I was **bitten** by your dog.*

In the passive voice, it is as if the object of the sentence suddenly gets a voice of its own and can describe an event from its own point of view. This applies even when it is inanimate:

> ACTIVE: *Henderson & Co demolished the old chapel.*
> PASSIVE: *The old chapel was demolished by Henderson & Co.*

The transformation from active to passive works like this:

SUBJECT   ACTIVE VERB   OBJECT

SUBJECT   PASSIVE VERB   'by' AGENT

For example:

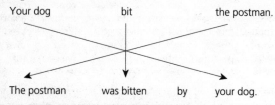

Your dog   bit   the postman.

The postman   was bitten   by   your dog.

WRITING TIP: active or passive?

General usage

Advocates of 'plain English' urge that writers should avoid the passive voice. It certainly has a number of disadvantages, of which the main two are:

1. It tends to sound rather formal and remote:
   The grass in the park should not be walked on.

2. It can lead to rather convoluted expressions:
   Improvements in the government grant to this and other NGOs were sought at the very highest level.

Sentence 1 would be better and simpler as:

   Do not walk on the grass in the park.

Sentence 2 would begin to become simpler if it were made active:

   We worked at the very highest level for improvements to our government grant—and that to other NGOs.

Sometimes, however, it is useful to avoid the more personal touch of the active voice and to use the more impersonal passive voice:

   Unfortunately your brother was run over by a speeding car.

continued ▶

Many would find this preferable to:

>   *Unfortunately a speeding car ran your brother over.*

which is more direct, but also more brutal.

By changing the voice between active and passive, we change the subject. This, in turn, means that the focus of the sentence shifts—in the example above it shifts from the car to the brother.

It + passive

A common usage is to begin a sentence with *it*, followed by a passive. For example:

>   *It is considered that you have no cause for complaint.*

Here the writer is trying to avoid responsibility, by refusing to use the active and give the verb a subject. (Compare: 'I do not think that you have any reason to complain.') Such usage is mealy-mouthed.

On the other hand, the construction may be quite useful:

>   *It is believed that the escaped man is still on the island.*

The writer may well not have a clear idea of exactly whose opinion is being quoted, although it is quite clear that the belief is widespread. In such a case the use of *It* + passive is useful.

FACTBOX: Phrasal and prepositional verbs

Phrasal verbs

A phrasal verb is made up of a verb plus an adverb. Phrasal verbs can be intransitive or transitive. For example:

INTRANSITIVE	TRANSITIVE
come round	bring up
fall apart	call off
lie down	lay down
roll over	mix up
stand out	put off

continued ▶

The adverb in transitive phrasal verbs can often come either before or after the object:

> *The union called the strike off.*
> *The union called off the strike.*

If the object is a personal preposition, then it usually precedes the adverb:

> *My mother brought me up.*

If the object is an extended noun phrase it is usually more convenient to place it after the adverb:

> *James put off his meeting with my parents.*

Prepositional verbs

These consist of a verb followed by a preposition. For example:

account for   look at   see to   worry about

It may seem difficult to distinguish between phrasal verbs and prepositional verbs, since some words can be both prepositions and adverbs (for example 'off'). The distinction is that the preposition of a prepositional verb must be followed by a noun, pronoun or noun phrase. So all prepositional verbs are transitive. In addition, the object must come after the preposition. So while it is correct to say:

> *He was looking at the notice.*

you cannot say:

> **He was looking the notice at.*

Linking verbs

As we saw in Chapter 2 some sentences consist of a subject and a verb followed by a **complement**. This is a sentence element that completes the subject. These are examples:

SUBJECT	VERB	COMPLEMENT
She	*became*	*a special constable.*
Her parents	*were*	*very pleased.*

The verbs used in such sentences belong to a small group of
linking (or 'copular') verbs. The commonest by far is 'be'. Others
are:

> *seem   appear   become   look*

Some of these can be used in other ways. For example 'appear' can
be used as an intransitive verb, in sentences such as:

> *A ghost suddenly appeared.*

Auxiliary verbs

Auxiliary verbs work with the main verb to complete the verb
phrase. They are:

be	is	am	are	was	were	been
have	has	had				
shall	will	should	would			
can	could					
may	might					
must						
ought (to)						

Auxiliaries break down into two sub-groups:

Primary auxiliaries

These are the verbs 'be', 'have', and 'do'. They have a dual function.
They work as auxiliaries:

> *The company **is** losing a lot of money.*
> *They **have been** losing money for some time.*
> *I **do** not approve of sex outside marriage.*

They can also stand on their own as main verbs in the sentence:

> *Mrs Jacobs **is** our new Publicity Manager.*
> *She **has** a lot of experience in this field.*
> *My new car can **do** over 100 mph.*

FACTBOX: *Do*

Main verb
As a main verb *do* has a wide range of meanings, for example:

- work at, perform
  What are you doing?
  The amateur drama group are doing 'The Prime of Miss Jean Brodie' next month.

- deal with
  Go upstairs and do your hair!

- attain, achieve
  He was clocked doing over sixty in a built up area.

Auxiliary
Its main auxiliary uses are:

- **to make negative statements**
  Unfortunately we just did not agree.

- **to form questions**
  Do you agree?

- **to form tag questions following statements in the simple present and simple past tenses**
  They live in the same street as you, don't they?
  I met you at Goodwood last year, didn't I?

- **for emphasis**
  I do hate it when they speak like that!

- **to avoid repetition**
  They keep their house a lot cleaner than we do.

This avoids having to say, 'They keep their house a lot cleaner than we keep our house.' There is more about this in the section on 'Ellipsis' on pp 131–3 in Chapter 11.

Modal auxiliaries

All the other auxiliaries in the list are described as 'modal'. Primary auxiliaries refer to actual events in the past or present; modal auxiliaries refer not to actual events, but to possible events. Some of them give us information about the speaker's views on the likelihood of something happening. Compare these statements:

> The job **will** be finished tomorrow.
> The job **may** be finished tomorrow.
> The job **can** be finished tomorrow.
> The job **might** be finished tomorrow.
> The job **could** be finished tomorrow.

Other modals enable us to express views on the desirability of an event:

> The job **should** be finished tomorrow.
> The job **ought** to be finished tomorrow.
> The job **must** be finished tomorrow.

FACTBOX: Types of verb

Verbs can be categorised as follows:

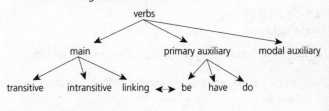

WRITING TIP

It is possible to express very subtle shades of meaning by using different modal auxiliary verbs. Compare the differences in meaning between the following sentences:

> I **can** see you tomorrow.
> I **could** see you tomorrow.
> I **may** see you tomorrow.
> I **might** see you tomorrow.

It is important to ensure that you choose the right word for the job.

continued ▶

can/may

Traditionally 'can' is used to indicate:

- **ability**

  I **can** speak Russian.

- **possibility**

  It **can** happen, you know.

'May' indicates:

- **permission**

  Ticket-holders **may** enter without further payment.

- **possibility**

  Accidents **may** cause delays.

Increasingly, however, 'can' is also used to indicate permission:

> Please **can** I leave the room?

'May' is rarely used in speech and tends to be used in formal or academic writing. If in doubt, however, follow the 'traditional' guidelines above.

may/might

'May' and 'might' are sometimes confused. 'May' is generally used for situations which remain open:

> Michael Smith may have become the best paid musician in the county.

'Might' is used when some or all of the possibilities have been closed off:

> Michael Smith might have become the best paid musician in the county. (Meaning that it's possible, but not very likely.)

> But for his untimely death, Michael Smith might have become the best paid musician in the county. (Meaning that it hadn't happened before he died and it is now impossible.)

Sometimes, however, you come across sentences like this:

> If it hadn't been for Michael Smith's untimely death he may have become the most successful musician in the county. (Which combines the actual, the possible and impossible in an impossible way!)

If the event referred to is now impossible, you should always use 'might' rather than 'may'.

Chapter 6:
Tense and 'tense'

In this chapter you can read about:

- **Tense and 'tense'**
- **English 'tenses' and aspects**
- **What English 'tenses' mean**
- **'Tense' and time**

Tense and 'tense'

We can change the form of the verb to indicate when an event happened. For example, we use the past tense form to indicate that something happened before 'now' and is therefore 'past':

> They **finished** the job yesterday.

Modern grammar normally uses the word 'tense' to mean just this: inflecting, or changing the form of, the verb word in order to indicate a change of time. On this basis, English only has two tenses: present and past. Surprisingly, it has no future tense. 'But of course it has a future tense!' you may object. 'What about "they will finish"?' Strictly speaking, this isn't a tense at all, because the stem of the verb has not changed; you have just added the modal auxiliary 'will' to it. And this is how English makes its great variety of 'tenses': by adding auxiliaries. The complete verb phrase, consisting of one or more auxiliaries plus the stem, present participle, or past participle of the main verb, constitutes the 'tense', which in other languages is a genuine single-word tense. So 'vous irez' in French translates into 'you will go' in English; if the one is a tense, then for practical purposes, the other is too. So in this book we refer to these, too, as tenses, but to distinguish them from the strict grammatical sense, the word is enclosed in inverted commas: 'tense'.

Tense and aspect

English has subtle and sophisticated ways of not just indicating the time of an event—past, present, future—but also of giving other information about it as well. This is done through the 'aspect' of the verb phrase.

It can be simple:

> *I walk*

continuous:

> *I am walking*

perfect:

> *I have walked*

or perfect continuous:

> *I have been walking*

Each provides a very different gloss on the action of walking, as is shown in these examples:

> *I walk to work every day.*
> *I am walking to work now.*
> *I have walked to work every day for the last twenty years.*

Table of English 'tenses' and aspects

	SIMPLE	CONTINUOUS	PERFECT	PERFECT CONTINUOUS
PAST	I walked	I was walking	I had walked	I had been walking
PRESENT	I walk	I am walking	I have walked	I have been walking
FUTURE	I shall walk	I shall be walking	I shall have walked	I shall have been walking

Active and passive

All 'tenses' can occur in the passive voice, but some are fairly uncommon:

	SIMPLE	CONTINUOUS	PERFECT	PERFECT CONTINUOUS
PAST	I was bitten	I was being bitten	I had been bitten	I had been being bitten
PRESENT	I am bitten	I am being bitten	I have been bitten	I have been being bitten
FUTURE	I shall be bitten	I shall be being bitten	I shall have been bitten	I shall have been being bitten

In addition to the basic 12-tense 'kit' there are all the possibilities offered by the use of other modals. For example:

> *I can walk, I can be walking, I could walk, I could have walked, I could have been walking*
>
> *I should walk, I should be walking, I should have walked, I should have been walking*
>
> *I must walk…*

and so on and so on.

What do English 'tenses' mean?

The twelve 'tenses' offer a very wide range of meanings, which native speakers of English largely take for granted but which foreign learners sometimes find bewildering. What follows is a simplified version of the main uses of each 'tense'.

Simple present: 'I walk'

1. **actions or states that are currently true but have no particular time reference**
   Peter lives in Troon.

2. **habitual actions**
   We visit Manchester once a month.

3. **timeless truths**
   The sun rises in the east.

4. **feelings and thoughts**
   I feel rather sad about that.
   (This is an event occurring at the time of speaking, but, unusually, does not require the present continuous—see below.)

5. **open conditionals**
   If I see her tomorrow, I'll mention it.

6. **scheduled future actions**
   Next week we go to Edinburgh on Monday, Perth on Tuesday and Inverness on Wednesday.

7. **newspaper headlines**
   PM meets Union bosses

8. **(occasionally) narrative**
   This man goes into a newspaper shop and asks for a cup of tea.

9. **in newspaper and other reviews**
   At this point in the story the hero realises his mistake.

10. **in commentaries**
    Peters crosses, Blake shoots, it's a goal!

Present continuous: 'I am walking'

1. **actions that are going on now but which are of a temporary nature**
   I'm speaking to you from a phone box at Gatwick airport.

2. **actions continuing over a period including the present, but of a temporary nature**
   He's working at Stratford all this week.

3. **habitual actions (again regarded as possibly temporary)**
   They're seeing a lot of each other.

4. **actions planned for the future**
   I am starting work at Bentons next week.

5. **describing a personal habit regarded as regrettable**
   I'm talking too much.

Present perfect: 'I have walked'

1. **completed past action with results lasting into the present**
   I have finished my work for today.

2. **series of completed past actions with results lasting into the present**
   I have warned her every day for the past week—but to no effect.

Present perfect continuous: 'I have been walking'

1. **completed past action with results lasting into the present, but with an emphasis on the fact that it went on over a period of time**
   — *Where have you been?*
   — *I've been walking the dog.*

Simple Past: 'I walked'

1. **completed action in the past**
   Rain stopped play.

2. **sequence of completed actions in the past**
   Our representative called at the house every day for a fortnight.

3. **conditionals**
   If he met me in the street he always said 'Hullo'.

Past continuous: 'I was walking'

1. **action in the past with emphasis on the fact that it was on-going**
   She was reading a book.

2. **This use is often contrasted with a simple past:**
   He phoned while she was reading a book.

Past perfect: 'I had walked'

1. **completed action in the past, often contrasted with one which came after it**
   When they had finished their coffee they paid the bill and left.

2. **sequence of completed actions in the past which came before a single completed action in the past**
   The athlete had stumbled several times before he fell full-length.

3. **conditionals**
   If I had received your letter I would have replied.

Past perfect continuous: 'I had been walking'

1. **continuing action in the past contrasted with a single completed action in the past**
   After we had been walking for some time, I realised that we were lost.

2. **a similar use, but referring to a sequence of past actions**
   Her boss had been criticising her for her mistakes for several weeks before she finally resigned.

Simple future: 'I shall/will walk'

1. **future action showing intention**
   I'll do it straightaway.
   They'll finish the job next week.

2. **general truths**
   In that kind of situation people will think first about their own safety.

Future continuous: 'I shall/will be walking'

1. **future action with emphasis on the fact that it is on-going**
   This time tomorrow I shall be walking in the Lake District.

Future perfect: 'I shall have walked'

1. **completed action in the future, usually with relevance to a particular future moment**
   By twelve o'clock we shall have walked ten kilometres.

Future perfect continuous

1. **completed action in the future, usually with relevance to a particular future moment, but with emphasis on the fact that the action will have gone on for some time**
   By twelve o'clock we shall have been walking for three hours.

'Going to' future

It is also common to use 'going to' plus the verb stem to express future meanings:

1. **general plans or intentions**
   They're going to invite her over next week.

2. **predictions**
   That car is going to crash.

WRITING TIP: *shall/will*

Sometimes it is not clear whether one should use 'shall' or 'will'. The rule of traditional grammar was as follows:

■ Normally use 'shall' with 'I' and 'we'. Use 'will' with all other persons.

■ Reverse this for emphasis, as in the famous example, 'I will do it and nobody shall help me.'

Increasingly, however, 'will' has become common in all uses. Indeed 'shall' is by far the least common of all the modal auxiliary verbs: for every occasion when 'shall' is used in conversation, 'will' is used fourteen times. The only common occurrence of 'shall' with 'I' and 'we' is in questions:

   Shall I phone you later?

The alternative, 'Will I phone you later?' is also possible, but in British English tends to be a regional rather than a general usage.

Tense and time

We have, so far, assumed that tenses are used to show time, and to some extent that is true. 'I walked' normally refers to the past, and 'I shall walk' to the future. But as we have seen in the preceding analysis, tenses can be used in a wide variety of ways. A clear example is the so-called 'present' tense. What we call the simple present tense is not often used to talk about an action taking place in the present. For that we normally use the present continuous:

> *I am walking along the High Street. I am talking to you on my mobile phone.*

We can use the simple present to refer to events that are actually going on as we speak, but only for special purposes, such as a live commentary:

> *I lift the saucepan carefully from the cooker and place it on a heat-resistant mat...*

More frequently we use this tense to refer to habitual actions:

> *I walk to work every day.*

and general truths:

> *Water freezes at 0 degrees Celsius.*

But we can also use it to refer to the future:

> *We fly to Moscow tomorrow.*

We can even use it to refer to the past:

> *This feller goes into a pub. 'Hey' he says to the landlord...*

So although it is true to say that verb tense can tell us about time, it is also important to remember that the time of an action is often determined by the other words in the sentence. In particular we frequently use time words and phrases to show when an action occurred:

PAST	PRESENT	FUTURE
yesterday	today	tomorrow
last year	this year	next year

Chapter 7:
More about clause patterns

In this chapter you can read about:

- **subjects**
  nouns as subjects
  pronouns as subjects
  noun phrases as subjects

- **objects**
  nouns as objects
  pronouns as objects
  noun phrases as objects
  reflexive pronouns as objects
  direct and indirect objects
  ditransitive verbs

- **complements**
  subject complement
  object complement

In Chapter 2 the idea of clause components and clause patterns was introduced. The three commonest clause patterns were described:

- SUBJECT + VERB
  They escaped.

- SUBJECT + VERB + OBJECT
  We saw them.

- SUBJECT + VERB + COMPLEMENT
  I was sad.

In this chapter, the clause components already introduced (subject, verb, object, complement) are examined further, and two more clause patterns are described. This involves an element of 'revision', so as to key in the new material.

The remaining clause component and patterns are covered in Chapter 8.

Subject

The subject usually comes at or near the beginning of the clause, and before the verb. In the simple sentences that follow, the subjects are printed in bold type.

> **The news from Albania** *continues to be bad.*
> **Journalists** *are still being arrested.*
> **Miriam** *came to see us yesterday.*

Sometimes the subject is a single word, like 'journalists' and 'Miriam'. Sometimes it is a group of words, like 'the news from Albania'. In each of the sample sentences, the subject gives us a good idea of what the sentence will be about. This is usually true, but not always. For example:

> **They** *saw the match on Wednesday.*

Here the subject is a **pronoun** which refers to someone or something else, so unless we know to whom it refers, we haven't a clear idea of what the sentence is about.

Sometimes we begin a sentence with a subject that gives absolutely nothing away:

> **It** *is raining.*
> **There** *is a fly in my soup.*

'It' and 'there' don't help at all; they are just words we use to form a particular kind of sentence. We could remove them and rearrange the words to express the same idea, but it wouldn't form a normal colloquial English sentence:

> *Raining is. (Or 'Is raining.')*
> *A fly is in my soup.*

WRITING TIP

English speakers normally put the subject of the sentence somewhere near the beginning. Sometimes we want to provide other information before it:

Before my last birthday	*my wife and I*	*went to London for the weekend.*
OTHER INFORMATION	SUBJECT	REST OF SENTENCE

There's no problem with this, provided we don't make the reader wait too long for the subject. If we do, then either patience runs out or confusion sets in…or both. In this example the subject is in bold, to help:

> *Several weeks before my last birthday, probably somewhere around 16th May, or thereabouts, certainly not during that very wet and windy April, **my wife and I** went to London for the weekend.*

So you should try to avoid putting too many words before the subject of the sentence. If you find yourself doing this, break the sentence into two parts, and put the additional information into one or more separate sentences:

> *Several weeks before my last birthday, my wife and I went to London for the weekend. I can't remember the exact date, but it was probably around 16th May, and certainly not during that very wet and windy April.*

What can be a subject?

If the subject of the sentence is a single word, it is usually a noun or a pronoun:

Nouns as subjects

In these examples the subjects, in bold, are all **nouns**.

> ***Harold** has started wearing a kilt.*
> ***People** have started to talk.*
> ***Kilts** are not very common in Chichester.*

Pronouns as subjects

In these examples the subjects, in bold, are all **pronouns**.

> **I** *have found a lot of holes in the lawn.*
> **They** *were made by rabbits.*
> **Some** *are quite deep.*

Noun phrases as subjects

If the subject is a group of words, it is usually a noun phrase. In these examples the subjects, all in bold, are **noun phrases**.

> **Some of her best friends** *are Americans.*
> **Very few of her American friends** *come from Baltimore.*

FACTBOX: The subject

The subject of a statement sentence usually:

■ comes at or near the beginning of the sentence

■ comes before the verb

The subject often, but not always, tells us what the sentence is about.
The subject of a sentence can be:

■ a noun

■ a pronoun

■ a noun phrase

Object

The object of a statement sentence normally comes after the verb. It refers to something or someone different from the subject. The exception to this is clauses in which the object is a reflexive pronoun (see 'Reflexive pronouns', below).

In the following sentences the objects are printed in bold type:

> *My brother-in-law does not eat **meat**.*
> *He cannot stand **it**.*
> *Instead he eats **a variety of vegetables**.*

What can be an object?

Objects are similar to subjects; they can be:

■ a noun
*My brother-in-law does not eat **meat**.*

■ A pronoun
*He cannot stand **it**.*

■ A noun phrase
*Instead he eats **a variety of vegetables**.*

Pronouns as objects

When personal pronouns are used as the object of a sentence they frequently change their form. This is because some personal pronouns have two forms: subjective and objective.

SUBJECTIVE	OBJECTIVE
I	me
we	us
he	him
she	her
they	them

The following personal pronouns only have one form:

■ you

■ it

WRITING TIP: *I* and *me*

People sometimes make mistakes about the use of I and me. You frequently hear sentences such as this:

> *They invited my husband and I to their house.*
> *Between you and I, this was a mistake.*

This usually happens when the object is a phrase ('my husband and I') which includes the personal pronoun. The mistake is easier to see if you reduce the phrase to the single pronoun:

> *They invited I to their house.*

Then the mistake is obvious.

Informally, 'me' is sometimes used as the subject of a sentence:

> *Me and my friend went to the meeting yesterday.*

Again if you reduce the phrase to the single pronoun, the mistake is clear:

> *Me went to the meeting yesterday.*

_I_ is only used for the subject. _Me_ is used for the object, and after prepositions.

Reflexive pronouns

Normally the object refers to a different person or thing from the subject. There is one exception to this rule, however. Some transitive verbs can describe actions that you can do to yourself. For example:

> *blame   free   introduce   kill   cut   hurt   surprise*

So we can say, for example, 'The teacher blamed Peter,' or 'The teacher blamed herself.' The pronouns used in sentences like these are called **reflexive pronouns**, and end in '-self' or '-selves'.

Direct and indirect objects

It is possible to have a sentence which contains two objects. In the following sentences these are marked as OBJECT 1 and OBJECT 2.

> *The managing director offered*   *David*   *a salary rise.*
>   OBJECT 1   OBJECT 2
>
> *Mary kept*   *her brother*   *a place in the queue.*
>   OBJECT 1   OBJECT 2

In each of these sentences both objects refer to someone or
something different from the subject. Each object, however, is
affected in a different way by the action referred to in the verb. In
each case we can say that object 1 receives or benefits from object
2: David receives the salary rise; Mary's brother benefits from the
place in the queue. So each of these is only an **indirect object**,
whereas in each sentence object 2 is the **direct object**, since it is
directly affected by the action of the verb:

> *The managing director offered* *David*   *a salary rise.*
>   INDIRECT OBJECT   DIRECT OBJECT
>
> *Mary kept*   *her brother*   *a place in the queue.*
>   INDIRECT OBJECT   DIRECT OBJECT

Sentences that contain an indirect object as well as the direct
object can frequently be transformed as is illustrated in the
following diagram:

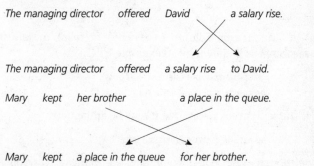

> *The managing director*   *offered*   *David*   *a salary rise.*
>
> *The managing director*   *offered*   *a salary rise*   *to David.*
>
> *Mary*   *kept*   *her brother*   *a place in the queue.*
>
> *Mary*   *kept*   *a place in the queue*   *for her brother.*

Ditransitive verbs

Verbs which can take two objects, direct and indirect, are called
ditransitive. As can be seen from the examples above, sentences
containing such verbs can often be transformed: some verbs use
'to' when the sentence is transformed, and others use 'for'. There
is also a group of verbs which can use both 'to' and 'for'.

> **FACTBOX: Prepositions used when transforming sentences containing common ditransitive verbs**
>
> | **1** | **2** | **3** |
> |---|---|---|
> | *to* | *to/for* | *for* |
> | award | bring | buy |
> | feed | leave | perfect |
> | forward | play | find |
> | give | take | fix |
> | grant | write | get |
> | hand | | keep |
> | lend | | make |
> | offer | | order |
> | owe | | prepare |
> | pass | | save |
> | pay | | set |
> | post | | |
> | read | | |
> | sell | | |
> | send | | |
> | show | | |
> | teach | | |
> | tell | | |

With the verbs in Column 2 the choice of 'to' or 'for' affects the meaning, as is shown by an example:

> *The assistant wrote a letter to his boss.*
> *The assistant wrote a letter for his boss.*

If the sentence is re-ordered it may be ambiguous:

> *The assistant wrote his boss a letter.*

(Although most people would take this to mean, '…wrote a letter to his boss.')

Which form of sentence?

Sometimes the choice of which sentence form to use is completely open. There is little to choose, for example, between these two sentences:

Mary kept her brother a place in the queue.
Mary kept a place in the queue for her brother.

At other times one form seems more or 'natural' than another. For example, it seems easier to say:

The managing director offered David a salary rise.

than:

The managing director offered a salary rise to David.

although here this is largely a matter of style. There is, however, one situation where a more general rule exists. When the direct object is a pronoun, such as 'it' or 'them', it is normal to use the sentence pattern with 'to' or 'for'. For example:

She gave it to me.

rather than

She gave me it.

and

The carpenter made it specially for me.

rather than

The carpenter made me it specially.

Complement

The grammatical term 'complement' is related to the verb 'complete'. The subject complement completes the meaning of the subject. The object complement does the same for the object.

Subject complement

In a sentence which contains a subject complement, the complement and the subject refer to the same person, thing, or idea. A complement, therefore, contrasts with an object, which refers to a different person, thing, or idea from the subject. In the following sentences the subject complement is printed in bold type.

*Mrs Washington is **our new managing director**.*
*The Directors were **delighted**.*

In sentences like these the verb acts like an = sign:

> *Mrs Washington = our new managing director.*
> *The Directors = delighted.*

Verbs of this type are described as **linking verbs.**

FACTBOX: Linking verbs

By far the commonest of these is: *be*
Others include:

appear	feel	look
prove	seem	smell
sound	become	get
grow	remain	

Some of these are also used as intransitive verbs. (For example: 'Only the silence remained.') Some are also transitive. (For example: 'get', 'prove', 'sound', 'grow', 'feel', 'smell'.)

The following types of the word and phrase can act as a subject complement:

■ noun
  My favourite writer is **Shakespeare.**

■ pronoun
  That book is **mine.**

■ noun phrase
  Mrs Washington is **our new managing director.**

■ adjective
  Mrs Washington was **happy.**

■ adjective phrase
  She became **rather embarrassed.**

Object complement

An object, too, can have a complement. In the following sentences the object complements are printed in **bold** type.

*The news made Peter **very happy.***
*The voters elected Senor Perez **president.***

In this type of clause, it is as if the words 'to be', or an equal sign, have been inserted between the object and its complement:

*The news made Peter (to be) **very happy.***
*The news made Peter = **very happy.***
*The voters elected Senor Perez (to be) **president.***
*The voters elected Senor Perez = **president.***

A range of meanings can be conveyed using suitable verbs and object complements:

- Causing
*That music next door is driving me **crazy.***

- Appointing
*They made him **a vice-chairman.***

- Naming
*Some people call him **a leader of fashion.***

- Expressing opinion
*Other people consider him **vain.***

FACTBOX: Verbs used with object complements

causing	appointing	naming	expressing opinion
drive	appoint	call	consider
get	crown	christen	think
make	elect	dub	
render	make	name	
send			
turn			

Chapter 8:
Adverbials

In this chapter you can read about these topics:

- **Sentences with obligatory adverbials**
  SUBJECT + VERB + ADVERBIAL
  SUBJECT + VERB + OBJECT + ADVERBIAL

- **Sentences with optional adverbials**

- **What can be used as an adverbial**
  adverb
  adverb phrase
  noun phrase
  prepositional phrase

- **Meanings and use of adverbials**
  adding information
    when?
    where?
    how?
    why?
    how much?
  adding focus
  conveying attitude
  linking parts of a text together

The story so far···

We have looked at four clause components:

- SUBJECT
- VERB

- OBJECT
  which subdivides into:
  - □ direct object
  - □ indirect object

- COMPLEMENT
  which subdivides into:
  - □ subject complement
  - □ object complement

These can be combined into five basic patterns:

```
SUBJECT  +  VERB
She          departed.

SUBJECT  +  VERB       +  COMPLEMENT
She          was           sad.

SUBJECT  +  VERB       +  OBJECT
She          caught        the train.

SUBJECT  +  VERB       +  INDIRECT OBJECT    +  DIRECT OBJECT
She          gave          the ticket collector   her ticket.

SUBJECT  +  VERB       +  OBJECT             +  COMPLEMENT
It           made          her                   unhappy.
```

In these five patterns, every element is obligatory—if you take
away any of them you destroy the structure of the sentence. You
can, of course, add other components which provide additional
information, as we shall see. But such additional elements are not
obligatory; if you remove them you reduce the amount of
information, but the sentence remains grammatically complete.

Introducing adverbials

There are a further two patterns which cover a small number of
sentences, where again every element is necessary.

Subject + verb + adverbial

As we saw in Chapter 4, verbs which do not require an object are
described as **intransitive**. The verbs in the following sample
sentences are examples:

> *The dog **disappeared***.
> *Maria **was singing***.

There is a small number of intransitive verbs which cannot stand on their own, but must be followed by something else. Each of the following 'sentences' is incomplete:

SUBJECT	VERB
The train	*hurtled…*
We	*live…*

In order to complete them we have to add one or more words:

SUBJECT	VERB	ADDITIONAL COMPONENT
The train	*hurtled*	***past***.
The train	*hurtled*	***down the track***.
We	*live*	***here***.
We	*live*	***in East Croydon***.

The component that has been added is called an **adverbial**. Intransitive verbs that always or frequently need to be followed by an adverbial include verbs of movement, such as:

> come   go   run   travel   walk

and verbs of position, like:

> lie   live   remain   sit   stand   stay

Subject + verb + object + adverbial

There is also a small number of transitive verbs (verbs that take an object), which need more than just an object. The following 'sentence' is incomplete:

SUBJECT	VERB	OBJECT
He	*put*	*the book…*

In order to complete it we need to add a further component:

SUBJECT	VERB	OBJECT	ADDITIONAL COMPONENT
He	*put*	*the book*	*away*.
He	*put*	*the book*	*on the table*.

Again the component that has been added is an **adverbial**. Transitive verbs that always or frequently need to be followed by an adverbial include verbs that refer to moving or positioning an object, such as:

> bring   lay   place   put   send   store

Ditransitive verbs, such as 'give' are also often used in clauses with an obligatory adverbial:

> *She gave that present* **to me**.

There is more about this in Chapter 7 on pages 76–9.

Optional adverbials

Obligatory adverbials are much less common, however, than those which are optional. The five main sentence patterns listed at the beginning of the chapter can all have adverbials added to them. In the following sample sentences, the adverbials are in bold type:

SUBJECT	+ VERB	+ **ADVERBIAL**		
She	departed	**on Saturday**.		

SUBJECT	+ VERB	+ COMPLEMENT	+ **ADVERBIAL**	
She	lived	happily	**ever after**.	

SUBJECT	+ VERB	+ OBJECT	+ **ADVERBIAL**	
She	caught	the train	**with minutes to spare**.	

SUBJECT	+ VERB	+ INDIRECT OBJECT	+ DIRECT OBJECT	+ **ADVERBIAL**
She	gave	the ticket collector	her ticket	**quickly**.

SUBJECT	+ VERB	+ OBJECT	+ COMPLEMENT	+ **ADVERBIAL**
It	made	her	unhappy	**all day**.

As can be seen from the examples, the adverbial is not an obligatory part of these sentences, it simply **adds** information, which is why some grammars refer to adverbials of this type as 'adjuncts'.

Position

In the previous examples, the adverbials were added at the end of the sentence, which is by far the commonest position for them. But adverbials can also occur at the beginning of the sentence:

> *At last she caught the train.*

They can also occur in the middle:

> *She finally caught the train.*

This is not to say that they can crop up *anywhere* in the sentence. You can't, for example, place an adverbial between the verb and its object, a mistake commonly made by foreign learners of English:

> *She caught finally the train.*

If an adverbial occurs in the middle of the sentence, it normally comes before the verb:

> *She finally caught the train.*

or between the auxiliary and the main verb:

> *She had finally caught the train.*

What can be an adverbial?

As we have seen, an adverbial can be a single word, or a group of words.

Single word

Normally if the adverbial is a single word, that word is an adverb:

> *He ran away.*
> *He ran easily.*
> *He ran fast.*

Occasionally, however, it is possible to use a noun as an adverbial:

> *Tuesdays we go to Leeds.*

but this is an informal usage.

FACTBOX: Adverbs

Adverbs form a word class, as do nouns, adjectives, and verbs. They are used as sentence adverbials, but they also have another important function. They can be used to **intensify** adjectives. In each of the following adjective phrases, the adverb intensifiers are printed in bold type:

> **very** *happy*
>
> **fairly** *pleased*
>
> **rather** *sad*
>
> **quite** *unusual*

As the examples show, intensifying adverbs can increase or decrease the power of the adjective they modify. In some cases (eg 'quite') they can allow the speaker to 'sit on the fence'. Only qualitative adjectives can be intensified in this way. Classifying adjectives cannot be preceded by an intensifier.

Adverbs can also be modified by an intensifier in a similar way:

> **very** *quickly*
>
> **fairly** *slowly*

and so on.

It is also possible to use short noun phrases as intensifiers. For example: *a* **bit** *sad*.

FACTBOX: Adverb formation

Adjectives can be transformed into adverbs by the addition of the suffix -ly. The rules for this transformation are these:

1. Normally just add -ly to the adjective
   sad ⟶ *sadly*

2. If the word ends in -ll, add -y:
   full ⟶ *fully*

3. Words of more than one syllable ending in -y, remove the -y and add -ily:
   happy ⟶ *happily*

continued ▶

4. Most single syllable words ending in -y just add -ly, except for:
   daily, gaily

5. Words ending with a consonant followed by -le, remove the final -e and add -y:
   terrible → terribly

A number of adjectives cannot be transformed into adverbs:

- There are a few adjectives that themselves end in -ly, for example *friendly*. These are not normally transformed by adding -ly (since 'friendlily' is rather awkward). Instead, use a phrase: *in a friendly way*.

- Most classifying adjectives (eg *French, metallic*).

- Most colour adjectives.

- Certain qualitative adjectives referring to very common qualities (eg *big, small, fat, little, young, old*).

Groups of words as adverbials

Three types of phrase can be an adverbial:

- an adverb phrase
- a noun phrase
- a prepositional phrase

Adverb phrase

In an adverb phrase, the main word, the headword of the phrase, is an adverb. The other words modify the adverb headword. They often come before the headword, as in the following examples:

MODIFIER(S)	HEADWORD
very	quickly
really rather	slowly

Occasionally they can come after the headword:

HEADWORD	MODIFIER
quickly	enough

Sometimes an adverb phrase can contain modifiers both before and after the headword:

MODIFIER	HEADWORD	MODIFIER
very	quickly	indeed

Noun phrase

It is also possible to use a noun phrase as an adverbial:

> I visited her **last year**.
>
> **Several times in the past few years** there have been serious accidents on that corner.

Prepositional phrase

By far the commonest phrase to be used as an adverbial is the prepositional phrase. This is a group of words with a preposition as its headword. The preposition always comes at the beginning and is followed by a noun, a pronoun, a noun phrase or the -ing form of a verb:

> He threw it **at John**. (PREPOSITION + NOUN)
>
> They did it **for me**. (PREPOSITION + PRONOUN)
>
> I found her **under the old oak tree**. (PREPOSITION + NOUN PHRASE)
>
> She only realised **after leaving**. (PREPOSITION + -ING FORM OF VERB)

Prepositions and prepositional phrases are covered in more detail in Chapter 4 on pages 40–3.

Meanings and uses of adverbials

Adverbials have three uses:

1. They add information to the sentence. Used in this way, adverbials are sometimes referred to as **adjuncts**.

2. They tell us about the writer's or speaker's attitude, and provide a 'commentary' on the text. Used in this way, adverbials are sometimes referred to as **disjuncts**.

3. They help to link clauses or sentences together. Used in this way, adverbials are sometimes referred to as **conjuncts**.

The first use is by far the commonest, accounting for around 90 per cent of all the adverbials we use.

Adding information

Typically adverbials provide the answers to the questions:

■ When?

■ Where?

■ How?

■ Why?

■ How much?

In addition some adverbials can add focus to the meaning of the sentence.

When?

Many adverbials give information about time:

■ **Position in time**
   *They arrived **at midnight**.*

■ **Duration**
   ***For several agonizing seconds** she stared into my face.*

■ **Frequency**
   *Last year they only won **three times**.*

■ **Relationship of two events**
   *That was **just after my birthday**.*

Common time adverbs are:

afterwards	today	tomorrow	yesterday
already	daily	earlier	ever
finally	first	frequently	hourly

continued ▶

immediately	last	later	monthly
never	next	now	often
presently	seldom	shortly	sometimes
soon	still	suddenly	then
usually	weekly	yearly	yet

Prepositional phrases used as time adverbials often start with:

after	at	before	by	during
for	from	in	on	since
throughout	to	until		

Where?

Many adverbials give information about place:

- **Position in space**
  I'll meet you **outside the library**.
- **Direction**
  The car was travelling **towards Leeds**.
- **Distance**
  The driver was unable to control the car **for several hundred yards**.

Common place adverbs are:

above	abroad	ahead	along	away
back	backwards	behind	below	beyond
clockwise	close	down	downstairs	east
forwards	here	home	indoors	inland
inside	left	near	nearby	north
nowhere	off	opposite	out	outdoors
outside	overhead	overseas	right	round
sideways	somewhere	south	there	underground
underneath	upstairs	west		

It is much more common, however, to use prepositional phrases, starting with words such as:

above	across	against	along	among
around	at	before	behind	below
beneath	beside	between	beyond	by
down	in	inside	near	off
on	outside	past	through	under
up	upon			

As you can see from these two tables, a number of prepositions can also stand on their own as adverbs of place. Examples are: *above, behind, out, round*.

How?

Many adverbials give information about manner. For example:

> The train was moving **very slowly**.
> He moved around **like a robot**.
> She spoke **with a strong Scottish accent**.

Many adverbs describing manner are formed by adding -ly to adjectives.

Why?

A number of adverbials can loosely be said to answer the question 'Why?' The kinds of meaning they convey are:

■ **Cause/reason**
  *Some people are suspicious of the company **because of its recent actions**.*

■ **Purpose**
  *He only does it **for the money**.*

■ **Condition**
  ***In the event of bad weather** the match will have to be cancelled.*

■ **Concession**
  ***Despite all our efforts** we were unable to save the game.*

It is very difficult to find adverbs that can act as adverbials answering the question 'why'. These adverbials are nearly always noun phrases, prepositional phrases, or clauses.

How much?

Certain adverbials allow the writer to modify the message of the sentence by telling the reader to what extent something is true:

> The share price has gone up **by 70 per cent**.
> I understand this **completely**.
> It only affected the result **slightly**.
> I don't mind **a bit**.

There are a number of adverbs which can be used in this way. For example:

altogether	completely	considerably	hardly	quite
rather	slightly	somewhat	totally	utterly

Focus

Some adverbials are used to focus attention on an element within the sentence:

> Many people find Turkish difficult. Basque is **also** a difficult language to learn.

Here the speaker is adding Basque to a list of languages that are difficult to learn, so the adverb 'also' helps focus our attention; it adds information. Notice that you can't achieve the same effect if you put 'also' at the beginning of the sentence:

> Many people find Turkish difficult. **Also** Basque is a difficult language to learn.

That sentence would only work in a different sequence:

> The Basque people live in a relatively isolated part of Europe. **Also** Basque is a difficult language to learn.

Other examples of sentences with focusing adverbials are:

> My uncle, **in particular**, has a wide range of interests.
> Soon **only** Britain will remain outside the Euro zone.

USAGE TIP: *also*

'Also' is an adverb and not a conjunction, although it is sometimes used instead of 'and':

> *She wrote a number of articles about ecology, also a children's information book.*

This is lazy writing and slightly confusing; the writer should have re-cast it as:

> *She wrote a number of articles and a children's information book about ecology.*

or:

> *She wrote a number of articles about ecology and a children's information book.*

depending on which is meant.

USAGE TIP: The position of adverbials

An adverbial can often be inserted in more than one place in a sentence. Sometimes the position of the adverbial makes little difference to the meaning and is a matter of style or emphasis. At other times, however, changing the position of the adverbial changes the meaning of the sentence:

> *The politician explained **with angry gestures** why he had left the meeting.*
> *The politician explained why he had left the meeting **with angry gestures**.*

It is particularly important to be careful about the placing of focusing adverbials like 'only'. Each of the following sentences has a different meaning:

1. ***Only** David has heard today's news.* (No one else has.)

2. *David has **only** heard today's news.* (He hasn't read it or seen it on TV.)

continued ▶

3. *David has heard **only** today's news.* (He hasn't heard yesterday's.)

It is worth pointing out, however, that in speech, example 2 is commonly used for meaning 3. In speech we can use stress and intonation to emphasise our meaning.

Adverbials to convey attitude

It is possible to comment on the information in a sentence in a variety of ways. In particular you can indicate your view of:

■ the facts themselves

■ your attitude towards them

■ the way in which you want to be regarded by your readers or listeners

Adverbials of this kind are sometimes called 'disjuncts'.

Attitude to the facts

You can use a range of adverbials to *limit the application* of the facts. For example:

> **In effect**, he gave in.
> All theories have to be modified in the light of experience **to some extent**.

To see the effect of these adverbials you only have to read the sentences without them. Common adverbials used in this way are:

almost	in a manner of speaking
in a way	in effect
more or less	practically
so to speak	to all intents and purposes
to some extent	up to a point
virtually	

It is also possible to comment on **how likely, possible, or real** the facts are. For example:

> *In theory you can dictate straight into your computer.*
> *In practice the software is still far from perfect.*

Common adverbials used in this way are:

actually	allegedly	apparently	certainly
definitely	doubtless	in fact	in practice
in reality	in theory	maybe	no doubt
officially	ostensibly	perhaps	possibly
presumably	probably	really	seemingly
theoretically	undoubtedly		

How you want your readers to think of you

You can 'personalise' your message by adding adverbials such as 'frankly' to a sentence:

> *Frankly, the match was a disaster.*
> *Quite honestly, I've never seen anything like it in my life.*

Adverbials used in this way are:

frankly	honestly	in my opinion
in my view	in retrospect	on reflection
personally	to my mind	truthfully

Adverbials for linking

Adverbials used to link sentences or parts of sentences are sometimes called 'conjuncts'. They are an important tool for giving a written text cohesion—they 'stick it together'. In the following short paragraph the linking adverbials are printed in bold:

> *There are several reasons for the country's economic decline. **Firstly** it had a base of traditional agriculture and little industry. **Then** the*

*governing class had little interest in business, being more concerned with the professions. **Also** the climate did not help, since the high average temperatures and rainfall made food readily available. This situation was not without its advantages, **however**.*

This topic is developed more fully in Chapter 11, on pages 133–6.

Chapter 9:
Multiple Sentences

In this chapter you can read about these topics:

- **Simple and multiple sentences**
- **Compound and complex sentences**
- **Co-ordinating clauses, phrases, and words**
- **Using co-ordinators**
- **Subordination**
- **Noun clauses**
  as subject, object, subject complement, object complement
  after certain adjectives
  in sentences beginning with 'It'

So far all the analysis in this account of English grammar has been based on simple sentences: sentences that consist of one finite clause. A clause is a group of words based on a verb phrase. It normally contains a subject and a verb phrase, and may also contain one or more additional components such as an object or an adverbial. A finite clause is one which contains a finite verb, that is to say a verb with a form that shows tense, and, in the present tense, number and person.

We call such one-clause sentences 'simple', but that is not to say that they are short or that they necessarily have simple meanings. Compare the following sentences:

> The cat sat on the mat.
> The large and rather vicious moggy given to us last week by a doting grandchild should not have been sitting on the Persian carpet in the living room.

Both are simple sentences, since each only has one finite verb: 'sat' in the first, and 'should have been sitting' in the second. Both follow a similar basic pattern of SUBJECT + VERB + ADVERBIAL, although the second has a number of other elements added. But whereas the first consists of six words, the second has 28; and while the meaning of the first is 'simple', the second requires considerably more concentration from the reader. Nevertheless, in grammatical terms, both are classified as simple sentences.

Multiple sentences

A sentence that consists of two or more finite clauses is described as a multiple sentence. Most everyday texts pitched at anything but the simplest level of comprehension contain a mixture of simple and multiple sentences. In the following paragraph the finite verbs have been printed in bold and the sentences separated to make it easier to spot the simple and multiple sentences.

> Seamen have always **dwelt** on the fringes of settled society.
>
> The Greeks **hesitated** whether to count them among the living or the dead, and eighteenth-century Englishmen **were** not much better **informed**.
>
> They **were** familiar with seafarers only as the inhabitants of modern European cities **are** familiar with tourists.
>
> They **recognized** their curious clothes and eccentric behaviour, they **laughed** at their oddities, they **profited** from their ignorance—but they **did** not **understand** seamen, and they **knew** nothing whatever of the world from which they **came**.
>
> Superficially familiar, the seaman **remained** to his contemporaries profoundly strange. They **knew** him only on land, out of his element.
>
> The sailor on a run ashore, probably drunk and riotous, **was** a popular image, but the sailor afloat and at work **was** quite unfamiliar to his countrymen.
>
> It **is** striking that almost all the prints of sailors **show** them in their flamboyant shore-going rig, never in their working clothes, nor at work.
>
> The shipboard world in which officers and men **spent** their active lives **was** probably less well known to men of education than the remote countries described in the travel books then so popular, or the remote ages on whose history they **had been brought** up.

Of these nine sentences three are simple and six are multiple. They range from the simple sentence, 'Seamen have always **dwelt** on the fringes of settled society,' to the complicated multiple sentence, 'The shipboard world in which officers and men **spent** their active lives **was** probably less well known to men of education than the remote countries described in the travel books then so popular, or the remote ages on whose history they **had been brought** up.'

Compound and complex sentences

Multiple sentences are classified according to the way in which their clauses are joined together. The simplest way of combining clauses into multiple sentences is by 'bolting them together', using words like 'and':

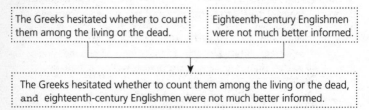

Sentences that contain clauses combined in this way are called **compound** sentences.

It is also possible to combine clauses by making one clause a component of the other, so that one clause forms the subject, object, complement or adverbial of the other—or sometimes just a part of the subject, object etc.

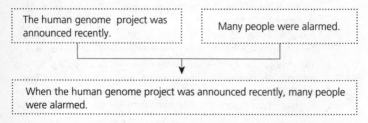

In this sentence the clause 'When the human genome project was announced recently' operates as an adverbial in the sentence as a whole. We could replace it with an adverbial consisting of a single word or a phrase and the structure of the sentence would not be altered:

ADVERBIAL	SUBJECT	VERB
When the human genome project was announced recently, (ADVERBIAL CLAUSE)	many people	were alarmed.
At the announcement of the human genome project recently, (PREPOSITIONAL PHRASE ACTING AS ADVERBIAL)	many people	were alarmed.
Recently (ADVERB)	many people	were alarmed.

This type of sentence is described as **complex**, which is, of course, a description of its **structure**, not its meaning. Complex sentences can have simple or complicated meanings, just like any other type of sentence.

FACTBOX: Types of sentence

Sentences can be:

■ **simple**
  containing only one finite clause

■ **multiple**
  containing more than one finite clause

Multiple sentences can be:

■ **compound**

■ **complex**

this relationship is shown in the following diagram:

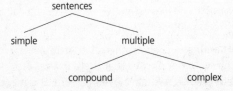

Compound sentences and co-ordination

In a compound sentence, the clauses are of equal value, grammatically speaking. The process by which they are joined together is called **co-ordination** and the words used to combine them are known as **co-ordinators**, or **co-ordinating conjunctions**.

The commonest co-ordinating conjunctions are:

> *and   but   nor   or   then   yet*

Of these, *and* is, unsurprisingly, by far the commonest, followed by *but* and *or*.

An important difference between compound and complex sentences is that the links between clauses in compound sentences don't do much more than join them together. They don't tell us much about the relationship between the clauses they join. The conjunction 'and' tells us nothing at all. A sentence like this:

> *Jane missed the meeting and the renewal of her contract was discussed.*

doesn't tell us whether the two pieces of information it contains are related and, if so, how. It could mean:

> *Although Jane missed the meeting, the renewal of her contract was discussed.*

or

> *Because Jane missed the meeting, the renewal of her contract was discussed.*

And these two sentences are clearly very different in meaning!

Other co-ordinating conjunctions do give a little more information. Compare this pair of sentences:

> *Jane missed the meeting and the renewal of her contract was discussed.*
> *Jane missed the meeting but the renewal of her contract was discussed.*

The first is ambiguous about the relationship between the two clauses; the second indicates that there is a relationship and implies that Jane should have been present at a meeting at which her contract was discussed.

Co-ordinating words and phrases

Of course we can use the same conjunctions within a clause to co-ordinate words:

> *We reached home tired **but** happy.*

or phrases:

> *Questions of discipline will be handled by the Deputy Head, **or** the Head of Lower School.*

FACTBOX: Co-ordination

Co-ordination means linking items of equal grammatical status using conjunctions. The co-ordinating conjunctions are:

and   but   nor   or   then   yet

You can co-ordinate:

- words: *bread **and** butter*

- phrases: *at your place **or** at mine*

- clauses: *I visited his house **but** I didn't see him.*

WRITING TIP: Using co-ordinators

Co-ordinating conjunctions can cause the writer a number of problems:

1. Normally co-ordinators should link items that are grammatically equivalent. For example, it is rather awkward to link a phrase and a clause:

> *He told us about his findings so far and that he still had several more areas to investigate.*

This would be better rephrased as:

> *He told us about his findings so far and the further areas to be investigated.*

continued ▶

2. *either/or, neither/nor*

Again these should link items of equal status. In particular you need to be careful where you place 'either' or 'neither' in relation to the verb. This is a common mistake:

The speaker neither explained what had happened nor why the accident had occurred.

The two items linked here are:

*explained what had happened
*why the accident had occurred

Moving 'neither' resolves the problem:

The speaker explained neither what had happened nor why the accident had occurred.

To check whether you have got it right, try removing the section of the sentence that begins with 'neither' (or 'either') and ends with 'no' (or 'or'). If the rest of the sentence works grammatically, then you are right:

The speaker ~~neither explained what had happened nor~~ why the accident had occurred. (WRONG)

The speaker explained ~~neither what had happened nor~~ why the accident had occurred. (RIGHT)

3. *either/or* and the agreement of the verb

a. If 'either' is the subject of the clause, then it is singular:
   I interviewed the two candidates again; either of them is suitable for the post.

b. When two singular items are linked using 'either'/'or' and together this phrase forms the subject, then the verb should be singular:
   Either Ms Grayson or Mr Howard is suitable for the post.

c. When a singular item is linked to a plural item using 'either'/'or' and together this phrase forms the subject, then the verb agrees with whichever is nearest to it:
   Either ice cream or chips are my favourite food.

continued ▶

> d. The same rule (of 'proximity') applies when the two subject items are pronouns of a different person:
>   *Either you or she is going to be invited to join us.*
> e. In informal usage, this is also often done when 'either' is used on its own:
>   *Either of the candidates are suitable for the post.*
>   In formal language, however, it is normal to use a singular verb:
>   *Either of the candidates is suitable for the post.*
>
> All these rules apply to 'neither' and 'nor'.

Complex sentences and subordination

A complex sentence contains one main clause and one or more subordinate clauses:

1. *When Sally arrived*   *the party really took off.*
   SUBORDINATE CLAUSE   MAIN CLAUSE

2. *The little boy went up to bed*   *as if he had lead weights on his feet.*
   MAIN CLAUSE   SUBORDINATE CLAUSE

3. *The minister told the waiting*   *that the announcement had*
   journalists   *been delayed.*
   MAIN CLAUSE   SUBORDINATE CLAUSE

In a complex sentence the subordinate clause forms one component of the main clause. In sentences 1 and 2 it is an adverbial. In sentence three it is the direct object. You can test this for yourself by substituting a word or phrase for the subordinate clause:

1. **Then**   *the party really took off.*

2. *The little boy went up to bed*   **slowly.**

3. *The minister told the waiting journalists*   **the news.**

> ### FACTBOX: Subordinate clauses
>
> Subordinate clauses relate to the main clause in a number of different ways:
>
> - They can act like noun phrases to form:
>   - subject
>   - object
>   - subject complement
>   - object complement
>
> - They can act as adverbials. (This is covered in detail in the chapter that follows.)
>
> - They can act as the modifier in a noun phrase. (This is described in more detail on pages 43–8)

Noun clauses

Noun clauses (sometimes called nominal clauses) do a similar job in the main clause to noun phrases. They can be:

- **Subject**
  What he said was quite amazing.

- **Object**
  You must decide what you want to do.

- **Subject complement**
  The building is not what it was.

- **Object complement**
  Naked ambition made her what she is today.

Notice that in each of these examples the noun clause can be replaced by a noun, pronoun, or noun phrase without changing the grammatical structure of the main clause:

> *It* was quite amazing
> You must decide *it*.
> The building is not *a palace*.
> Naked ambition made her *the winner*.

(Of course when the noun clause acts as a complement, it could also be substituted by an adjective or adjective phrase: 'The building is not **beautiful**', 'Naked ambition made her **unhappy**'.)

Noun clauses can be introduced by:

1. *that*

2. *what, why, when, where, how, whether, if*

Examples

SUBJECT	**When you go** is your decision.
	Whether they go or not is up to them.
	How William came to be king is the subject of my next lecture.
OBJECT	He told us **how he had escaped from prison**.
	I just don't know **when I should reply**.
	We thought **that you weren't coming**.
SUBJECT COMPLEMENT	The question is **whether the engine will last out to the end of the race**.
	Her problem is **where she left her key**.
	My aim is **that we should meet up in Edinburgh during the festival**.
OBJECT COMPLEMENT	The experience made the king **what he always should have been**.

More about noun clauses introduced by question words

what, why, when, where, how can all be used to introduce questions. For example:

> *What* did you do yesterday?
> *How* are we going to get there?

This gives a strong clue about how they are used to introduce a dependent clause in a complex sentence: there is a question involved. Often it is in the form of a piece of reporting:

> He asked me *what I did yesterday*.
> I wonder *how we are going to get there*.

In each case the subordinate noun clause is the object of the verb in the main clause. Similar clauses can be introduced by 'if' or 'whether':

> I wonder *whether we shall get there by lunchtime*.

The commonest verbs to be followed by such noun clause objects are:

    ask   know   remember   see   tell   wonder

Noun clauses introduced in these ways can also form the subject complement of the main clause:

> *Kingston is **where I went to school**.*
> *That is **how I knew you were coming**.*

They can also be its subject:

> ***What I don't understand** is how you knew I was coming.*

In this last sentence both subject and subject complement are noun phrases.

Clauses introduced by 'that'

1. By far the commonest of these are clauses that form the object of the main clause. Such 'that' clauses commonly occur after verbs such as:

       believe   feel   find   know   say   see   show
       suggest   think

   For example:

   > *The MP said **that he had never received cash for asking questions**.*

2. When a 'that' clause is used in the subject complement, it often follows an adjective. The typical pattern is:

   SUBJECT + '*be*' + ADJECTIVE + 'THAT' CLAUSE.

   The commonest adjective used in such sentences is 'sure'. For example:

   > *I'm sure **that you would agree with me**.*

   Here the noun clause is being used to modify the adjective 'sure'. (It could be said to answer the question, 'What kind of "sure" are you?' – 'I'm "That you would agree with me" kind of sure.')

Other typical adjectives are:

afraid	amazed	annoyed	astonished	certain	convinced
disappointed	glad	pleased	positive	relieved	sorry
surprised	worried				

3. A third way in which 'that' clauses are used is in sentences that begin with 'It'. For example:

> It never occurred to me **that you didn't know the full facts**.

Here the pronoun 'It' is being used as a dummy subject. Grammatically this is really a sentence on the pattern:

SUBJECT + VERB + ANOTHER CLAUSE ELEMENT, but if we arrange the words in that order the sentence becomes extremely awkward:

> That you didn't know the full facts never occurred to me.

Other examples of this pattern are:

> It follows that hydrogen must be present.
> It now appears that they were mistaken.

Such 'It' sentences often follow the pattern:

'It' + LINKING VERB + ADJECTIVE + 'that' CLAUSE

For example:

> It is strange **that you didn't meet him**.

Again, reversing the word order would be awkward:

> That you didn't meet him is strange.

Common adjectives used in this way are:

> clear   likely   possible   true

Others include:

amazing	astonishing	certain	crucial	disappointing
doubtful	essential	important	incredible	interesting
natural	obvious	odd	probable	sad
shocking	strange	surprising	vital	

WRITING TIP: Missing out *that*

It is possible to miss out *that* in any of these clauses without affecting the grammar or the meaning:

*The MP said **he had never received cash for asking questions**.*
*I'm sure **you would agree with me**.*
*It never occurred to me **you didn't know the full facts**.*
*It is strange **you didn't meet him**.*

What decides whether we do or do not use *that* to introduce such clauses is the situation. *That* is nearly always used in more formal situations, especially in academic writing, but its use in conversation is much less common.

FACTBOX: Noun clauses

Noun clauses function in a similar way to noun phrases. They are introduced by:

■ that, if, whether

■ what, who(m), why, when, where, how

They can be:

■ subject

■ object

■ subject complement

■ object complement

Clauses introduced by 'that' can also be used in two other ways:

■ to develop the meaning of adjectives like *afraid, sorry, sure*
  (*I'm sorry that they weren't here to meet you.*)

■ in sentences beginning with the dummy subject 'it'
  (*It annoyed me that she didn't answer my letter.*)

Non-finite clauses

So far in this book the emphasis has been on finite clauses, that is to say clauses which contain a finite verb. (A finite verb is a verb which is either in the present tense or the past tense. In the present tense it agrees with the subject in number or person. If the verb phrase contains more than one word, then the first word in it must be a finite verb.)

But it is also possible to construct non-finite noun clauses. These contain a non-finite part of the verb:

- **to** + VERB STEM
  to see   to go etc
  These are called **INFINITIVE CLAUSES**.

- **the -*ing* form of the verb**
  seeing   going etc
  These are called *-ING* **CLAUSES**.

Infinitive clauses

Infinitive clauses can act in the same way as noun phrases and can be:

- the **subject** of the main clause
  To err is human.

- the **object** of the main clause
  They want to succeed.

- the **subject complement** of the main clause
  The real problem is to win the first round.

They can also appear in sentences starting with *It* in a similar way to *that* clauses. Just as we can say

> *It never occurred to me that you didn't know the full facts.*

as a neater construction than

> *That you didn't know the full facts never occurred to me.*

So we can also say

> *It is easy to do that.*

instead of

> **To do that** is easy.

-ing clauses

These clauses can be:

- the **subject** of the main clause
  Eating ice-cream is my idea of heaven.

- the **object** of the main clause
  *They adore **ski-ing in Austria**.*

- the **subject complement** of the main clause
  *The real problem **is winning the first round**.*

Clauses that work like adjectives

Finite clauses that work like adjectives are to be found in noun phrases and are referred to as **relative clauses**. Non-finite clauses can be used in a similar way. This is described in Chapter 4 on pages 43–48.

Clauses that work like adverbials

We can use adverbial clauses to answer four of the basic questions that adverbials answer:

- **When?**
  *They arrived   **at midnight**.* (PHRASE)
  *They arrived   **just as the clock was striking twelve**.* (CLAUSE)

- **Where?**
  *They met   **at the cross roads**.* (PHRASE)
  *They met   **where they met before**.* (CLAUSE)

- **How?**
  *He moved   **like a robot**.* (PHRASE)
  *He moved   **as if he was powered by clockwork**.* (CLAUSE)

- **Why?**
  *He did it   **for the money**.* (PHRASE)
  *He did it   **so that he could get more money**.* (CLAUSE)

Adverbial clauses, however, have such a wide variety of forms and uses that they are tackled in detail in the following chapter.

Chapter 10:
Adverbial clauses

In this chapter you can read about the following types of adverbial clause:

- **Time**

- **Place**

- **Manner**

- **Reason**

- **Purpose**

- **Result**

- **Condition**

- **Concession**

- **Comment**

We saw in the previous chapter that adverbial clauses work like adverbials within a clause to answer the questions, 'When?', 'Where?', 'How?', and 'Why?'. These functions are covered in this chapter along with a number of other important features of adverbial clauses.

Time

We can use adverbial clauses to answer the question, 'When?'. **Temporal** clauses indicate the time relationship between two events: what happens in the main clause and what happens in a subordinate clause. Compare these two sentences:

> *The party ended after I left.*
> *After the party ended I left.*

There are two clauses:

> *the party ended   I left*

By arranging the sentence in two different ways, even though we use the same temporal conjunction 'after', we change the sequence of events.

Meanings

An adverbial clause of time can be used to describe events that happen:

- **before the event in the main clause**
  When she had completed her work she went home.

- **at the same time as the event in the main clause**
  While I was sitting on the bus I read a newspaper.

- **after the event in the main clause**
  She completed her work before she went home.

Conjunctions

Adverbial clauses of time are introduced by these conjunctions:

after	as	before	since
until	when	while	

WRITING TIP: Using *as* and *since*

These two conjunctions can be used to introduce clauses of time:

> ***As** I was going home I saw Mrs James.*
> *The attacks haven't happened again **since** she moved house.*

Both can, however, also introduce clauses of reason:

> ***As** it is Friday, we shall go home half an hour early.*

continued ▶

> *He was allowed to go free **since** the police had no evidence against him.*
>
> Sometimes it can be unclear which meaning is intended:
>
> > ***As** he was leaving to go to lunch he left the door unlocked.*
>
> Here it isn't clear whether he left the door unlocked *when* he left to go for lunch, or *because* he was leaving to go for lunch (ie he was planning to come back shortly). If there is a risk of this kind of ambiguity, consider using an alternative conjunction: *because* for reason and *when* for time.

Finite and non-finite clauses

All the examples given so far have been of finite clauses, but non-finite clauses are common. These frequently use the -ing form of the verb:

> *After completing her work she went home.*
> *While sitting on the bus I read a newspaper.*

It is also possible to convey similar meanings using prepositional phrases:

> *When she had completed her work*   *she went home.*
>
> ↓
>
> *After completing her work*   *she went home.*
>
> ↓
>
> *After the completion of her work*   *she went home.*

Place

Adverbial clauses of place answer the question, 'Where?'. They give information about the place where the event in the main clause occurred:

> *I found the keys where Sheila put them.*

Conjunctions

Conjunctions used to introduce adverbial clauses of place are:

where	wherever	everywhere

Note, however, that not all clauses introduced by these conjunctions are adverbial clauses. 'Where' is frequently used to introduce noun clauses. For example:

I know where I'm going.

The quick way to check what type of subordinate clause you are dealing with is to replace it with a single word or short phrase:

I found the keys ~~where Sheila put them~~.

I found the keys **there**.

Since 'there' is an adverb, the clause is an adverbial clause.

I know ~~where I'm going~~.

I know **that**.

'That' is a pronoun, so the clause must be a noun clause.

Manner

Adverbial clauses of manner answer the question 'How?'. They provide information about how the action described in the main clause was performed:

Why does Peter behave as he does?

We can also compare an action or a state with something else:

I feel as if a brick has been dropped on my head.

Conjunctions

Conjunctions used to introduce clauses of manner are:

as	as if	as though
just as	much as	

'Like' is also frequently used for this purpose, in sentences such as:

> *I feel like a brick has been dropped on my head.*

Such usage is, however, informal and is disapproved of by purists, who say that 'like' should be followed by a noun, pronoun, or noun phrase. In sentences like the example it should be replaced by 'as' or 'as if'.

Clauses of manner can also be introduced by '(in) the way (that)' in sentences such as:

> *The car is running in the way that it always has.*

Non-finite clauses

Non-finite clauses of manner can be introduced by 'as if' and 'as though'. These are then followed by 'to' plus the verb stem:

> *At the next jump the horse slowed, as if to steady itself.*

Verbless clauses

Verbless clauses can be introduced in a similar way:

> *He behaved as if in a trance.*

Reason

Adverbial clauses of reason answer the question, 'Why?'. They give an explanation of why the event or state described in the main clause occurred:

> *They signed the contract without reading it because they were in a hurry.*
> *Since it's Thursday she won't be in the office until ten.*

Conjunctions

The main conjunctions used to introduce clauses of reason are:

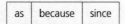

| as | because | since |

Purpose

Clauses of purpose also answer the question 'Why?', but they explain events or states in the main clause by referring to the intentions of one or more participants:

> *They signed the contract without reading it so that they could save time.*

Non-finite clauses

Non-finite clauses of purpose are often simpler to use than finite ones and are frequently preferred. They are introduced by 'to', or by a conjunction ending with 'to' followed by the verb stem:

> *They signed the contract without reading it to save time.*

Conjunctions

The conjunctions used vary according to whether the clause is finite or non-finite:

FINITE	NON-FINITE
in order that	in order to
so that	so as to
so	to

Result

These adverbial clauses provide information about the results of the state or action referred to in the main clause:

> *We arrived at the theatre late so we missed most of the first act.*
> *The train was so late that I missed my connection at Euston.*
> *I got such a shock that I dropped the plate I was holding.*
> *He spoke in such a way that even children could understand.*

Conjunctions

Result clauses can be introduced by:

so	and so
so that	so _ _ _ _ _ _ that
such (a) _ _ _ _ _ _ that	in such a way that

Non-finite clauses

The conjunctions above ending in 'that' have versions ending in 'as to' that are used to introduce non-finite clauses:

> *The goods were so expensive as to put them beyond the reach of ordinary people.*
> *The hall was left in such chaos as to make it useless for the next week.*

Condition

Conditional clauses enable us to make a variety of statements in which the truth or otherwise of the main clause is dependent on the truth of the subordinate clause:

> *If you don't stop doing that I shall call the police.*

Conjunctions

There are two conjunctions used to introduce conditional clauses: 'if' and 'unless'.

Meanings

Conditional clauses take a variety of forms and can convey a range of meanings.

Common events

We can use them to make statements of general truths. For example:

> *If the temperature rises above zero Celsius, ice begins to melt.*

In sentences of this type the verbs in both the main clause and the subordinate clause are in the simple present tense.

It is also possible to make such general statements about the past:

> *In those days, if a gentleman's honour was insulted, he 'demanded satisfaction'.*

Possible events

We can make statements about hypothetical but possible events in a similar way:

> *If the boss visits the factory he usually sacks someone.*

Here the grammatical structure is the same as for general truths: the use of the simple present in both clauses. It is also possible to use the present perfect in both clauses:

> *If the surveyor has been here, I haven't seen him.*

Specific statements about the future

A common use for conditional clauses is to speculate about possible future events:

> *If they come, he will give them a piece of his mind.*

Here the subordinate clause is in the simple present, while the main clause is in the future. This can be, as here, the simple future, with 'will' or 'shall', or it can be the 'going to' future:

> *If they come, he's going to give them a piece of his mind.*

It is also possible to use the present tense modal auxiliaries 'can' and 'may':

> *If they come, he can give them a piece of his mind.*

Sentences of this type leave the likelihood of the events described completely open: he may come, or he may not. If we consider that the future event is unlikely, then we can indicate this by changing the form of the verb:

> *If they came, he would give them a piece of his mind.*

In sentences of this type the verb in the subordinate clause is in the simple past, while the verb in the main clause is preceded by a modal auxiliary in the past tense, usually 'should' or 'would'. It is also possible to use 'might' or 'could':

> *If they came, he might give them a piece of his mind.*

In formal English you will also encounter the subjunctive:

> *If they were to come, he would give them a piece of his mind.*

But this usage is becoming increasingly rare, except in the so-called 'impossible' conditional:

> *If I **were** you, I would….*

Here 'were' is standard and 'was' is informal—and considered by many to be a mark of 'ignorance'.

Past conditionals

It is also possible to speculate about how things might have been in the past:

> *If he had come, I would have given him a piece of my mind.*

This, too, is impossible, since we now know that he didn't come and so the condition remained unfulfilled. In sentences of this type the subordinate clause has a verb in the past perfect tense.

Omission of 'if'

It is also possible to construct conditional clauses without the use of a conjunction. The commonest ways of doing this are to begin the clause with 'were', 'should', or 'had':

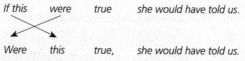

| *If this* | *were* | *true* | *she would have told us.* |

| *Were* | *this* | *true,* | *she would have told us.* |

Other examples are:

> *Should they agree to the new arrangement, the company would be back in business as early as next Tuesday.*
>
> *Had we known, we would have done something about it.*

Concession

In sentences which contain a clause of concession, there is some kind of contrast between the main clause and the subordinate clause:

1. The most obvious is in sentences beginning with 'although':

    Although she stumbled, she went on to win the race.

    Here the information contained in the main clause is surprising in the light of the fact(s) contained in the subordinate clause.

2. In other sentences containing concession clauses, the subordinate clause expresses something that is quite likely to be true, but which doesn't affect the truth of the main clause:

    Even if I come last in the race I shall still be proud to have taken part.

3. In a third type of sentence the subordinate clause expresses an exception which detracts from the truth of the main clause:

    I would have won except that I fell over my own feet.

Conjunctions

Concession clauses can be introduced by the following conjunctions:

although	despite	even if	even though	except that
much as	not that	though	whereas	while/whilst

Non-finite clauses

Non-finite clauses of concession can be introduced by one of the following conjunctions, followed by the -ing form of the verb:

(al)though	despite	in spite of	while/whilst

For example:

Despite stumbling, she went on to win the race.

Verbless

It is also possible to have verbless concession clauses. These are
formed by using a conjunction followed by an adjective, an
adjective phrase, or a noun phrase.

The conjunctions used are:

(al)though	even if	if	while/whilst

For example:

> Although **an inexperienced athlete,** she won the race easily. (NOUN
> PHRASE)
>
> Although **very inexperienced,** she won the race easily. (ADJECTIVE
> PHRASE)

Comment

In Chapter 6 we saw the various ways in which adverbials can be
used to comment on the meaning of the sentence as a whole.
Adverbial clauses can also be used for this purpose. They are
introduced by the conjunctions 'as', and 'as far as', in sentences of
this type:

> As far as I can see, the two statements are very similar to each other.

Other typical expressions are:

> as I understand it
> as is generally the case
> as _ _ _ _ _ _ _ _ _ _ said

Adverbial comment clauses are, by their nature, quite common in
speech – and are popular with politicians and other public figures!

Non-finite clauses

Comparable non-finite clauses include such expressions as:

> to be fair....
> broadly speaking....

Chapter 11:
Building texts

In this chapter you can read about:

- **Coherence, cohesion, and formal structure**
- **How cohesion is achieved in a text**
  referring words
  ellipsis
  sentence adverbials

So far we have focused entirely on how words can be combined into larger units which culminate in a sentence, following the pattern:

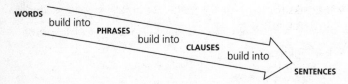

WORDS — build into — PHRASES — build into — CLAUSES — build into — SENTENCES

The process doesn't end there, however. Most communication doesn't take place as a series of single isolated sentences. Normally sentences form part of a **text**. By 'text' linguists don't just mean words written or printed on paper; they use the word to refer to any self-contained block of communication, from a telephone conversation to an encyclopaedia. The sentences that comprise a text are related to each other in three important ways:

- coherence
- formal structure
- cohesion

Coherence

The text has to make sense from sentence to sentence. It's no good starting with a sentence about nuclear physics and following it immediately with one about bee-keeping—unless, of course, you manage to show a clear link between the two. Coherence is provided by continuity of subject matter and the use of appropriate and related vocabulary. Most of the time we take it for granted and only tend to remark on its absence. 'He seemed a bit incoherent,' we may remark of a speaker, for example.

Formal structure

Many texts follow a formal structure which provides them with a pattern. The commonest of these in writing is the paragraph. This part of the book you are reading is written in **paragraphs**. Paragraphing makes written texts easier to read for a variety of reasons:

- It breaks the page up and makes it physically easier to find your way around.

- Paragraphs normally follow a similar pattern, which makes it easier for the reader to follow the writer's thought:

  - **topic sentence** introducing the main idea of the paragraph (and, frequently, linking it to the subject matter of the preceding paragraph);

  - **sentences which develop the topic sentence**;

  - **concluding sentence** that rounds the paragraph off (and often leads in to the next).

- This pattern also provides a useful structure and discipline for the writer.

There are other conventions covering both the written word (for example, the layout of a recipe) and the spoken (for example, a telephone conversation).

Cohesion

Cohesion is more subtle and takes rather longer to explain. It is the process by which we use grammar and vocabulary to 'glue' the sentences to each other and make it easier for the reader or listener to follow. It is achieved partly by the words we choose and the patterns of the text. Politicians and preachers, for example, are very fond of repetition. Direct repetition of words and phrases, and the use of synonyms and antonyms all help to give texts rhythm, pattern, and cohesion.

There is a limit to the extent to which such means can be used, however. A much commoner way of achieving cohesion is the use of grammatical devices. Until the advent of hypertext, all texts were essentially linear. Speech takes place in time and is a sequence of sounds building up to make units of sense. Writing, too, is experienced by the reader as a sequence. It is true that it is possible to stop reading and look back and ahead in the text, but essentially we read texts in sequence. Because both spoken and written texts are linear we need to be able to link the present sentence to those that have gone before and those which will come after. Such referring forward and backwards is called **deixis**. Referring back is **anaphoric deixis** and referring forward is **cataphoric deixis**, but they will be described in this book as 'referring back' and 'referring forward'.

The many different grammatical devices by which we can refer forwards and back in text can be placed into three groups:

- **Referring words**
  Certain groups of words enable us to refer clearly and briefly to what has gone before, or what is coming later without repetition.

- **Ellipsis**
  Certain constructions enable us to refer back to earlier material, while missing out sections of sentences without confusing the reader or listener. This process is called **ellipsis**.

- **Sentence adverbials**
  The types of adverbials called **conjuncts** and **disjuncts** are also

known as sentence adverbials (see pages 95–7). Conjuncts create links between sections of a text. Disjuncts allow the writer to comment on parts of a text and also contribute to its cohesion.

The paragraph you have just read contains a number of examples of how this works, which are illustrated in this diagram:

Refers back to last sentence in previous paragraph, especially 'Direct repetition . . . antonyms'	**A comparison like this implies what has gone before ('Commoner than what?').**

There is a limit to the extent to which such means can be used, however. A much commoner way of achieving cohesion is the use of grammatical devices. Until the advent of hypertext, all texts were essentially linear. Speech takes place in time and is a sequence of sounds building up to make units of sense. Writing, too, is experienced by the reader as a sequence. It is true that it is possible to stop reading and look back and ahead in the text, but essentially we read texts in sequence. Because both spoken and written texts are linear we need to be able to link the present sentence to those that have gone before and those which will come after. Such referring forward and backwards is called **deixis.** Referring back is **anaphoric deixis** and referring forward is **cataphoric deixis,** but they will be described in this book as 'referring back' and 'referring forward'.

'too' ties this sentence in to the last, since it is adding to the argument

'Such' compresses the meaning of these words from the previous sentence: 'link the present sentence to those that have gone before and those which will come after'.

Refers back to 'anaphoric deixis and cataphoric deixis'

Referring words

Pronouns

The commonest and most obvious words used to refer back are pronouns:

*The motorist tried to stop behind the police car at the traffic lights. Unfortunately **his** brakes failed and **he** collided with **it**.*

This is much simpler than:

> *The motorist tried to stop behind the police car at the traffic lights. Unfortunately **the motorist's** brakes failed and **the motorist** collided with **the police car**.*

Personal pronouns are used to refer back to:

- nouns
- noun phrases
- other pronouns

Demonstrative pronouns (*this/that/these/those*) are used in a similar way:

> *That evening they took us to Shipley to see their new house. This was a beautiful 18th century building just at the end of the High Street.*

Here the demonstrative refers to a specific noun phrase, 'their new house', but sometimes it is used to refer not to any particular noun or noun phrase, but rather to all the information contained in the preceding sentence:

> *The motorist tried to stop behind the police car at the traffic lights. Unfortunately his brakes failed and he collided with it. **This** was embarrassing.*

The relative pronoun 'which' can be used in a similar way:

> *The motorist tried to stop behind the police car at the traffic lights. Unfortunately his brakes failed and he collided with it. **Which** was embarrassing, to say the least.*

Determiners

In Chapter 3 we saw that noun phrases often contain one or more determiners coming before the noun:

DETERMINER(S)	NOUN
the	cat
all my seven	cats

Determiners can be used to state or imply a reference back in a text. For example, the use of 'the' in this text:

> *She owned several pets including a dog and five Siamese cats. **The** dog was an elderly Golden Retriever called Sam…*

In the following example the numeral 'three' serves a similar purpose:

> Our family consisted of five daughters. **Three** daughters lived in Esher.

Auxiliary verbs

Just as pronouns can stand instead of nouns and noun phrases, auxiliary verbs can stand in for the whole verb phrase, to avoid unnecessary repetition. This is described more fully in the section on ellipsis, but the use of 'do' in the following example is very common as a referring device:

> I had promised that I would visit them the following morning.
> Unfortunately I was unable to **do** so because of a problem with my car.

FACTBOX: so and such

These two words can be used in a variety of ways to add cohesion to a text.

So

1. **Referring back to the complement of a previous clause**
   *The monsoon has been unreliable or non-existent for several years and, with the advent of global warming, will probably remain **so**.*

2. **Preceded by if**
   *That should solve the problem. **If so,** please don't bother to reply.*

3. **After verbs like say, hope, think**
   *I wouldn't have believed the story if she hadn't told me **so** herself.*

Such

Such can be used as a determiner or as an adjective:

1. **Determiner**
   *She used to read a lot of horror stories and romantic novels. After a while she began to find **such** books unsatisfactory.*

2. **Adjective**
   *I began to receive visits from people trying to sell me all sorts of things I didn't want, from double glazing to garden gnomes. One **such** salesman returned on no fewer than five occasions.*

Other words and phrases

Especially in written texts, there are a variety of words and phrases a writer can use to signpost the argument or narrative:

> *The events referred to **above** were, in fact, only the beginning of a sad and tedious history which dragged on for several years. This is sketched in **below**.*

In this type of text there are many ways in which writers refer to and sum up what has gone before.

> *…he also pointed out that this was the first occasion on which such a failure had occurred.*
> *This **argument** proved very convincing to those present…*

Whole texts, or sections of text can be referred to using words like:

account	advice	answer	argument	charge
declaration	denial	demand	description	excuse
explanation	proposal	question	remark	report
statement	suggestion			

Similarly ideas can be referred to as, for example:

analysis	belief	fear	hope
idea	interpretation	opinion	plan
theory	view	wish	

WRITING TIP: Emotive content

When summing up an idea or a text in the ways suggested above it is possible to indicate to the reader your own opinion of it. It is possible to do this explicitly: the difference between calling an idea an 'interpretation' and calling it a 'misinterpretation' is obvious. Other alternatives are more subtle. An 'estimate' sounds much more thoughtful than a 'guess', for example, and to call an 'idea' a 'notion' tends to diminish it in the mind of the reader or listener.

> **FACTBOX: Referring words**
>
> We can refer backwards and forwards in a text by using:
>
> ■ PERSONAL PRONOUNS
>   *she, they* etc
>
> ■ DEMONSTRATIVE PRONOUNS
>   *this, that, these, those*
>
> ■ RELATIVE PRONOUNS
>   *which*
>
> ■ DETERMINERS
>   *the, three* etc
>
> ■ OTHER WORDS AND PHRASES
>   *former, latter, above, below* etc
>   *argument, opinion, notion* etc

Ellipsis

As we have seen, pronouns and other words enable us to refer to what has gone before (or what is yet to come) without repetition. When the verb remains the same in two sentences, or within one multiple sentence, it is possible to avoid repetition by missing out the main verb and just using an auxiliary. For example:

> *Parsons has written many more books than I have.*

Here the auxiliary verb 'have' stands in for the full verb phrase 'have written'.

There are several different occasions on which this can occur. Those which are listed here can occur in both speech and writing.

■ **Contrasting subjects**
  Mr Gray *next door cuts the grass much more often than* **I** *do.* (Words omitted: *cut the grass.*)

■ **Contrasting objects**
  She played **the cello** *with the same enthusiasm as she did* **tennis**. (Word omitted: *played.*)

- **Contrasting adverbials**
  *They met **in Bath**, not as they normally did **in Bristol**.* (Word omitted: *met*.)

- **'To be'**
  *She thinks she **is clever** and she **is**.* (Word omitted: *clever*.)

- **'To have'**
  *She asked if she **had a lump on her forehead**, and she **had**.* (Words omitted: *a lump on her forehead*.)

- **Using a modal**
  *She **doesn't check** her work as carefully as she **should**.* (Words omitted: *check her work*.)
  *I **could have saved** money but I **didn't**.* (Words omitted: *save money*.)

Ellipsis in speech

Conversation is frequently extremely elliptical:

> A: *I met an old friend of yours yesterday.*
> B: *Who?*
> A: *Beth.*
> B: *Where?*
> A: *The Radnor Arms.*

If you compare this with the 'complete' version, you can see why we use ellipsis:

> A: *I met an old friend of yours yesterday.*
> B: *Who did you meet yesterday?*
> A: *I met Beth yesterday.*
> B: *Where did you meet her?*
> A: *I met her at the Radnor Arms.*

FACTBOX: Ellipsis

Ellipsis occurs when one or more words are omitted from a text to avoid repetition. Typically it involves replacing a complete verb phrase by an auxiliary verb. It can also involve the omission of other clause components. Common occasions for ellipsis are:

continued ▶

- contrasting subjects, objects, or adverbials

  *She goes to Italy much more often than I **do***.

- use of the verbs 'to be' and 'to have'

  *I feared I had lost my wallet and I **had***.

- use of a modal auxiliary such as *could* or *should*

  *We haven't seen her as much as we **could***.

Ellipsis is common in spoken English.

Sentence adverbials

Conjuncts and **disjuncts** are used in a text to link different parts together. They work in a number of different ways:

- **Adding and listing**

  In narratives, explanations, and arguments we often want to place items in a particular order. We indicate this fact and show the order by using words like 'firstly':

  > *There were several reasons why the new marketing campaign was unsuccessful. **First** the advertising agency had misunderstood the brief. **Then** the weather was quite unseasonally hot, which made sales of woolly hats extremely difficult. **Finally** our competitors slashed their prices.*

Sometimes the sequence is less important, but we still wish to make it clear that items are linked:

> *The child had a succession of bad school reports. **Furthermore** she was caught shoplifting…*

Sentence adverbials used in this way include:

at the same time	finally	first	last
meanwhile	next	soon	then
also	as well	at the same time	besides
furthermore	in addition	moreover	too

■ **Giving examples**

Sometimes we wish to introduce an example or list of material which exemplifies part of the argument:

> *He had written several popular books about astrology, **for example:** 'What your stars foretell'.*

Other words used in this way are:

> *namely, as follows*

■ **Saying things another way**

We may also wish to restate something using different words:

> *Even when he was Managing Director, Sam was first and foremost a salesman. **In other words** he had little interest in production problems.*

■ **Cause and result**

In texts that contain an argument one sentence is often the logical development of what has gone before:

> *They were rather slow to produce a prototype and this proved much more expensive than had been expected. **As a result** the time and money available for development work were limited.*

Other sentence adverbials of this type are:

accordingly	as a result	consequently	hence
so	therefore	thus	

■ **Contrasts and alternatives**

A sentence can be contrasted with what has gone before:

> *The team has been remarkably unsuccessful this year, which is a cause for some concern. **On the other hand** they are still young and have a lot of latent talent.*

Other sentence adverbials of this type are:

all the same	alternatively	anyway	by contrast
conversely	even so	however	instead
nevertheless	on the other hand	rather	yet

■ **Concession**

Another type of contrast is similar to that used in adverbial clauses of concession: despite this fact, the following is true. For example:

> *The teacher was sure that she had counted all the children.*
> ***Nevertheless*** *when the coach got back to the school Liam was missing.*

Other sentence adverbials of this type are: 'however', 'yet', 'even so'.

WRITING TIP: *however*

The word *however* has a number of related uses:

- CONJUNCTION
  It is used to introduce an adverbial clause of manner:

  > ***However*** *it happened, we now have a disaster on our hands.*

- MODIFIER
  It can also be used with an adjective or adverb to introduce an adverbial clause of concession:

  > ***However*** *hard you try you will still not succeed.*

- QUESTION WORD
  It can be used as an emphatic version of 'How?':

  > ***However*** *did you do that?*

- SENTENCE ADVERBIAL
  It is used in a text to show a relationship between an earlier section and the current one:

  > *The two children saved up all their pocket money for several months. It was still not enough,* ***however***.

  When used like this it can also come at the beginning of the sentence:

  > *The two children saved up all their pocket money for several months.* ***However,*** *it was still not enough.*

The use of *however* as a sentence adverbial is largely confined to fairly formal texts, especially academic texts. The convention is to separate it from the rest of the sentence by a comma if it comes at the beginning or end of the sentence, or by a pair of commas if it comes in the middle of the sentence. This signals that it is being used as a sentence adverbial and not in some other way.

FACTBOX: Sentence adverbials

Sentence adverbials are words or short phrases used to show links between sections of a text. Different sentence adverbials indicate different types of link, of which the commonest are:

- adding and listing
  firstly, then, etc

- giving examples
  for example

- saying things another way
  in other words

- cause and result
  so, therefore, as a result

- contrasts and alternatives
  on the other hand

- concession
  however, nevertheless, yet, even so

Section B
Glossary and Usage Guide

abstract noun

Nouns are sometimes grouped by meaning into abstract and concrete. Abstract nouns are those which refer to feelings, ideas, and other mental constructs; concrete nouns refer to people, places, and things which can be experienced using the five senses:

ABSTRACT	CONCRETE
happiness	car
success	keyboard
truth	sand
beauty	tree

It is sometimes argued that, if possible, you should avoid using too many abstract nouns. While it is true that a text stuffed with abstracts can be longwinded and even difficult to read, the examples quoted show that the list of abstract nouns contains many words which are frequently used in ordinary speech. Avoiding them would be pointless and counterproductive.

active voice

Transitive verbs can be used in two different ways or 'voices': active and passive:

> ACTIVE: *The car **struck** her*.
> PASSIVE: *She **was struck** by the car*.

Transitive verbs usually refer to some kind of action. In the active voice the subject is the person, thing, or idea that performs the action. In the passive voice the subject is the recipient of the action.

The active voice is by far the more common of the two.

See also: **PASSIVE VOICE**

adjective

A class of words that refer to the qualities of people, things, and ideas, or which group them into classes. Most adjectives satisfy the following tests:

1. They modify a noun and are normally placed before it. This is described as their **ATTRIBUTIVE** function.

   *a **blue** flower, a **slow** train*

2. They can be the complement of the subject of a clause. This is described as their **PREDICATIVE** function.

   *The test was **positive**.*

3. They can be graded by adding a modifier before or after them:

   *a very **slow** train*
   *The results were **good** enough.*

4. They have a **COMPARATIVE** and **SUPERLATIVE** form:

   | sad | sadder | saddest |
   | unusual | more unusual | most unusual |

Not all adjectives satisfy all these tests, however. Some are only predicative and cannot be used before a noun. You can say 'She was **alone**', but not 'I saw an **alone** woman'. Others cannot be used predicatively. You can talk about 'an **atomic** bomb', but you cannot say 'the bomb was **atomic**'.

Adjectives can be divided into qualitative and classifying. **QUALITATIVE** adjectives give information about the qualities of a creature, thing, or idea ('a **tall** man', 'a **stupendous** idea'). **CLASSIFYING** adjectives place creatures, things, and ideas into categories ('the **French** connection', 'an **annual** occurrence'). Classifying adjectives cannot be graded (#3 above) and do not have comparative and superlative forms (#4 above).

adjective phrase

An adjective phrase is a group of words built up on an adjective headword. There are two ways in which this is commonly done:

One or more modifying adverbs are placed before the adjective:

She was | very | remarkable.

ADVERB | ADJECTIVE

ADJECTIVE PHRASE

Modifiers can also be placed after the adjective:

ADJECTIVE	MODIFIERS
slow	enough
intrigued	by her stupidity

adjunct

The category of **ADVERBIAL** that adds further information to the **CLAUSE**. Adjuncts can provide information about:

- **place**
  They met **on the beach**.

- **time**
  They met **at night**.

- **manner**
  They met **by accident**.

- **cause/reason**
  They met **because of a broken promise**.

- **purpose**
  They met **for old times' sake**.

- **condition**
  In the event of non-payment the goods remain the property of the company.

- **concession**
  Despite all my pleas, she went home alone.

- **degree**
  They didn't care **at all**.

adverb

A class of words. Adverbs frequently act as sentence **ADVERBIALS**, providing information about, for example, place, time, and manner. Examples are:

- **place**
  here, away, somewhere

- **time**
  soon, already, still

- **manner**
  easily, fast, slowly

They can also be used as **INTENSIFIERS**, combining with adjectives to make **ADJECTIVE PHRASES**:

> **very** easy, **rather** attractive

They also continue with adverbs, to make adverb phrases:

> **extremely** slowly, **very** fast

Adverbs can be formed from **QUALITATIVE ADJECTIVES** by adding -ly:

> easy + ly = easily

Not all adverbs, however, end in -ly.
See also: **ADVERB FORMATION**.

adverb formation

Adjectives can be transformed into adverbs by the addition of the suffix -ly. The rules for this transformation are these:

Normally just add -*ly* to the adjective.

> *sad* ⟶ *sadly*

If the word ends in -*ll*, add -*y*:

> *full* ⟶ *fully*

Words of more than one syllable ending in -*y*, remove the -*y* and add -*ily*:

> *happy* ⟶ *happily*

Most single syllable words ending in -*y* are regular, except for:

> *daily, gaily*

Words ending with a consonant followed by -*le*, remove the final -*e* and add -*y*:

> *terrible* ⟶ *terribly*

A number of adjectives cannot be transformed into adverbs:

There are a few adjectives that themselves end in -*ly*, for example *friendly*. These are not normally transformed by adding -*ly* (since 'friendlily' is rather awkward). Instead, use a phrase: *in a friendly way*.

Most classifying adjectives (eg *French, metallic*).

Most colour adjectives.

Certain qualitative adjectives referring to very common qualities (eg *big, small, fat, thin, little, young, old*).

Adjectives which have the same form as the adverb (eg *fast*).

adverb phrase

A phrase with an **ADVERB** as **HEADWORD**, with **MODIFIERS** before, or after, or both. For example:

> *very smoothly*
> *as economically as possible*

adverbial

A clause component (like **SUBJECT**, **VERB**, **OBJECT**, **COMPLEMENT**). Adverbials can be divided into:

- **adjuncts**
  These provide additional information.
  Examples: *slowly, at a snail's pace*

- **conjuncts**
  These are used to provide a link between sentences.
  Examples: *moreover, in addition*

- **disjuncts**
  These make comments on the information in one or more preceding sentences.
  Examples: *however, by contrast*

Adverbials can be a single word, usually an adverb, or a group of words:

- a prepositional phrase
  Examples: *at a snail's pace, in addition*

- an adverb phrase
  Examples: *very slowly, too quickly for me*

- a noun phrase
  Examples: *last Wednesday, several times today*

See also: **ADVERBIAL POSITION**

adverbial clause

In complex sentences, adverbial clauses can give information about:

- **time**

- **place**

- **manner**

- **reason/cause**

- **purpose**

- **condition**

- **concession**

There are separate entries for each of these in this glossary.

adverbial, obligatory

Most adverbials are optional; that is to say that they can be removed without affecting the grammatical structure of the clause. There are two clause patterns, however, in which the adverbials are obligatory; if the adverbial is removed, the clause is no longer grammatically viable.

1. SUBJECT + VERB + ADVERBIAL
   There is a small group of **INTRANSITIVE** verbs which are normally followed by an adverbial. The group includes:

   belong, come, go, lie, live, run, sit, stand, stay, travel, walk

As can be seen, these are all verbs referring to movement or position. They are normally followed by adverbials of place. For example:

> *That book belongs **to me**.*
> *She was lying **on the ground**.*

2. SUBJECT + VERB + OBJECT + ADVERBIAL
   There are a few transitive verbs where the object has to be followed by an adverbial. The following verbs, for example, normally have an adverbial after the object:

   > direct, lay, lead, place, point, put, set, tie, throw

   As can be seen, these are all verbs referring to moving or positioning something. They are normally followed by adverbials of place. For example:

   > *The officer directed the car **down a side road**.*
   > *I placed the gift **on a low table**.*

adverbial, optional

In most sentences the adverbials can be removed without altering the grammatical structure; so they can be described as 'optional'. In a few cases, however, adverbials are obligatory.

adverbial position

Adverbials can come at the beginning or end of a clause:

> ***After several hours of negotiation** a deal was struck.*
> *A deal was struck **after several hours of negotiation**.*

This doesn't mean that you can always use either of these positions for any adverbial. For example, this is possible:

> *She did her shopping **at great speed**.*

But this is not:

> ***At great speed** she did her shopping.*

Adverbials, especially single word (**ADVERB**) adverbials, can also be placed in the middle of the clause, normally before the verb:

> *They **finally** reached home.*

or between the **AUXILIARY** and the **MAIN VERB**:

> *They have **finally** reached home.*

Adverbials can not, however, be placed between the verb and its object.

after

This word has two main uses:

- **SUBORDINATING CONJUNCTION** used to introduce an adverbial clause of time:
  *I only knew her **after** she was elected.*

- **PREPOSITION**
  *I only knew her **after** her election.*

after/afterwards

'After' is a preposition which should be followed by a noun, pronoun, or noun phrase:

> *We reached home very late **after** the party.*

'Afterwards' is an adverb of time:

> *We saw a film and had a meal **afterwards.***

'After' should not be used as an adverb, although it sometimes is:

> *We saw a film and had a meal after.*

agreement

The subject and verb of a clause agree in number and person:

SUBJECT	VERB	REST OF SENTENCE	
I	am waiting	for a bus.	1ST PERSON SINGULAR
Mary and I	are waiting	for a bus.	1ST PERSON PLURAL
Peter	is waiting	for a bus.	3RD PERSON SINGULAR

Another name for agreement is 'concord'.

See also: **PERSON, NUMBER**

also

'Also' is an adverb and not a conjunction, although it is sometimes used instead of 'and':

> *The Minister received visits from the ambassadors of several Asian countries, also the editor of* The Times.

This is lazy writing and slightly confusing; the writer should have re-cast it as:

> *The Minister received visits from the ambassadors of several Asian countries and the editor of* The Times.

anaphoric deixis

Referring back in a text.
  See DEIXIS

and

A CO-ORDINATING CONJUNCTION used to link together two grammatical features of equal status:

- **word**
  *bread **and** butter*
  *to **and** fro*

- **phrase**
  *our American allies **and** European neighbours*

- **clause**
  *She came in at about six **and** immediately started complaining about the state of the house.*

any

A word that can be used in a variety of ways:

1. **determiner**
   *You could lose the lot at **any** moment.*

2. **pronoun**
   *He asked her to lend him some money, but she told him she hadn't got **any** to spare.*

3. **adverb** (before the comparative of an adjective or adverb)

*If she drives **any** faster she'll crash.*

apposition

When a noun or noun phrase is placed up against another noun or noun phrase 'in parallel' it is said to be in apposition:

*The main speaker, **the Mayor of Southsea**, was over fifteen minutes late.*

The words 'the Mayor of Southsea' is doing exactly the same grammatical job as 'The main speaker' and either could stand alone as the subject of the sentence. Its purpose is to provide additional information to define the first noun phrase more precisely.

In the example above the information provided by the noun phrase in apposition is not essential to the noun phrase it is working with; if we remove it we do not disable the sentence. It is therefore 'non-defining'. It is also possible to have a defining noun phrase in apposition:

*The writer **George Orwell** was a socialist.*

Here, if we remove 'George Orwell' we take away what defines the subject of the sentence, and are left with:

The writer was a socialist.

which clearly doesn't make much sense on its own.

as

The word 'as' can be used in a number of different ways:

1. A **subordinating conjunction** used to introduce a range of adverbial clauses:

- TIME

  ***As** the train pulled in to the station I realised I'd lost my ticket.*

- MANNER

  *The bully reacted **as** bullies always do.*

- REASON

  ***As** Monday is a holiday the meeting has been postponed until Tuesday.*

■ COMMENT

As I understand it, you should have finished the work yesterday.

2. A **preposition**:

I took up a job as a teacher of music.

3. An **adverb**

He was as happy as a sandboy.

See also: LIKE/AS

as...as...

This useful construction can cause problems, because it is not always clear how the second 'as' is being used. Often there isn't a problem:

*Laszlo didn't play the second movement **as** well **as** Herman.*

Difficulties arise when you want to use a personal pronoun:

*She didn't play the second movement **as** well **as** me / I.*

The first 'as' is an adverb. The second may be either a conjunction, in which case the sentence should end with 'me'. Or it may be a conjunction so that the full form of the sentence would be:

*She didn't play the second movement **as** well **as** I did.*

Most people nowadays would probably say,

*She didn't play the second movement **as** well **as** me.*

The choice is one of style rather than sense. The construction *as...as...*can sometimes lead to ambiguity, however. For example:

*She doesn't visit Mary **as** often **as** George.*

This has two possible meanings:

*She doesn't visit Mary **as** often **as** she visits George.*
*She doesn't visit Mary **as** often **as** George does.*

If you wish to be clear, you need to spell it out.

attributive adjective

Most adjectives can be used to modify a noun. This function of adjectives is called attributive. Attributive adjectives are usually placed before the noun:

*a **happy** event   the **red** wheelbarrow*

A small number of adjectives can come after the noun they modify:

> the president **elect**

These are sometimes referred to as post-positive adjectives.

auxiliary verb

Auxiliary verbs work with the MAIN VERB to complete the verb phrase. They are:

be	is	am	are	was	were	been
have	has	had				
shall	will	should	would			
can	could					
may	might					
must						
ought (to)						

Auxiliaries break down into two sub-groups: PRIMARY AUXILIARIES and MODAL AUXILIARIES.

base

The word to which PREFIXes and/or SUFFIXes are attached to form new words.

before

This word has two main uses:

■ SUBORDINATING CONJUNCTION used to introduce an adverbial clause of time:
The accident occurred before it was light.

■ PREPOSITION
The accident occurred before 8 am.

but

A CO-ORDINATING CONJUNCTION used to link together two grammatical features of equal status:

■ **word**
tired but happy

■ **phrase**
useful at times but expensive to run

■ **clause**
They bought a new car but it immediately started to go wrong.

by

This preposition has a number of related but different meanings, so careless usage can produce results that are unintentionally comic:

> *My mother was knocked down **by** the police station.*
> *The tree that was struck by lightning is to be replaced **by** the Headteacher.*

Care is clearly needed.

can

'Can' is a **MODAL AUXILIARY VERB** used to indicate ability or possibility:

> *She **can** swim now.*
> *That **can** happen occasionally.*

See also: **CAN/MAY**

can/may

Traditionally 'can' is used to indicate:

■ **ability**
*I **can** speak Russian.*

■ **possibility**
*It **can** happen, you know.*

'May' indicates:

■ **permission**
*Ticket-holders **may** enter without further payment.*

■ **possibility**
*Accidents **may** cause delays.*

Increasingly, however, 'can' is also used to indicate permission:

> Please **can** I leave the room?

'May' is rarely used in speech and tends to be used in formal or academic writing. If in doubt, however, follow the 'traditional' guidelines above.

case

Certain pronouns change their form according to their use. They can be subjective, objective, or possessive:

SUBJECTIVE CASE	OBJECTIVE CASE	POSSESSIVE CASE
I	me	mine
we	us	ours
he	him	his
they	them	theirs
who	whom	whose

The subjective case is used for the subject of a clause and also in formal English for the subject complement. The objective case is used for the object of a clause and also after a preposition.

Nouns also change their form; they show possession by adding 's:

> The **company's** recent success

This is known as the 'possessive case' of the noun.

cataphoric deixis

Referring forwards in a text.
See: DEIXIS

cause, adverbial clause of

See: REASON, CLAUSE OF

cause, adverbial of

See: ADVERBIAL, ADJUNCT

classifying adjective

A type of adjective is used to place creatures, things, and ideas into categories. They include such words as:

> annual   Vietnamese   atomic

Adjectives that do this are described as 'classifying', since they place things into classes. They do not normally have comparative and superlative forms; you cannot, for example, say that one event is 'more annual' than another. Either an event is annual or it isn't. Classifying adjectives cannot normally be graded, either. They are contrasted in these respects with **QUALITATIVE ADJECTIVES**.
See also: **COMPARATIVE**, **GRADING**, **SUPERLATIVE**

clause

The grammatical level immediately below that of **SENTENCE**. A sentence may consist of one or more clauses. **DECLARATIVE** clauses normally have a **SUBJECT** and a **VERB**, and follow one of the basic **CLAUSE PATTERNS**. Clauses can be **FINITE** or **NON-FINITE**, according to whether or not they contain a finite verb. Sentences can consist of one or more finite clauses. They may also contain non-finite clauses. In the following sentences, the finite clauses are marked by boxes:

| Science is a mystery to many people | and | that is unfortunate. |

| While | they were waiting for the train | they saw Mrs Dalloway waiting on the other platform. |

The latter sentence also contains a non-finite clause:

| While they were waiting for the train they saw Mrs Dalloway | waiting on the other platform. |

See also: **ADVERBIAL CLAUSE**, **NOUN CLAUSE**, **RELATIVE CLAUSE**

clause elements

Clauses consist of five elements: **SUBJECT**, **VERB**, **OBJECT**, **COMPLEMENT**, **ADVERBIAL**. These can be arranged in seven basic **CLAUSE PATTERNS**.

clause patterns

All **DECLARATIVE** clauses follow one of seven basic patterns:

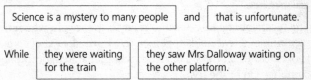

SUBJECT+VERB: *She*   *arrived.*
                 S   V

SUBJECT+VERB+OBJECT:	*She*	*met*	*her friend.*	
	S	V	O	

SUBJECT+VERB+INDIRECT OBJECT+DIRECT OBJECT

	He	*gave*	*her*	*some flowers.*
	S	V	Oi	Od

SUBJECT+VERB+OBJECT+ADVERBIAL

	He	*took*	*her*	*to the car.*
	S	V	O	A

SUBJECT+VERB+ADVERBIAL:	*They*	*went*	*into town.*
	S	V	A

SUBJECT+VERB+COMPLEMENT	*She*	*was*	*tired.*
	S	V	C

SUBJECT+VERB+OBJECT+COMPLEMENT

	The meeting	*made*	*her*	*happy.*
	S	V	O	C

INTERROGATIVE, IMPERATIVE, and EXCLAMATORY CLAUSES follow variants of some of these patterns.

coherence

The term coherence is used to refer to the way in which the meaning of a text holds together. We normally expect a text to show a common thread of sense, whether stated, or implied, or a combination of the two.

cohesion

The term cohesion refers to the way in which the elements of a text are linked together using vocabulary and grammatical means. The commonest grammatical elements that provide cohesion are:

- DEIXIS (referring forward and back)
- ELLIPSIS
- the use of CONJUNCTS and DISJUNCTS

See also REFERENCE.

common noun

Nouns can be divided into two groups: proper nouns and common nouns. All nouns that are not PROPER NOUNS are described as 'common'.

comparative and superlative

QUALITATIVE ADJECTIVES have three forms:

ABSOLUTE	bright	intelligent
COMPARATIVE	brighter	more intelligent
SUPERLATIVE	brightest	most intelligent

Words of one syllable add -er and -est to make the comparative and superlative. Words of three or more syllables don't add -er and -est, but are preceded by *more* and *most*. Two-syllable words vary: some add -er and -est and some use *more* and *most*. Confusingly, some do both.

complement

Part of a clause that completes the meaning of an earlier part. The subject complement completes the meaning of the subject; the object complement completes the meaning of the object.

Mrs Hope-Brown	is		*rather retiring.*
SUBJECT	VERB		SUBJECT COMPLEMENT
Meeting people	made	her	nervous.
SUBJECT	VERB	OBJECT	OBJECT COMPLEMENT

See also: **SUBJECT COMPLEMENT**, **OBJECT COMPLEMENT**

complex sentence

A sentence that contains a **MAIN CLAUSE** and one or more **SUBORDINATE CLAUSE**s, linked by subordinating conjunctions. Examples of complex sentences are:

SUBORDINATE CLAUSE	MAIN CLAUSE
When the sun came out	*they went into the garden.*
MAIN CLAUSE	SUBORDINATE CLAUSE
She told me	*what I wanted to know.*
SUBORDINATE CLAUSE	MAIN CLAUSE
If I were you	*I'd see a doctor about that rash.*

compound sentence

A sentence that contains two or more main clauses linked by co-ordinating conjunctions. Examples of compound sentences are:

MAIN CLAUSE	MAIN CLAUSE		MAIN CLAUSE
He came in,	*went straight to his desk,*	*and*	*started telephoning.*

	MAIN CLAUSE		MAIN CLAUSE
	Either you go	*or*	*I do.*

concession, adverbial clause of

There are three types of concession clause, but all show some kind of contrast between the main clause and the subordinate clause:

1. The most obvious is in sentences beginning with 'although':

    Although she always came top of the class, she failed her exams.

    Here the information contained in the main clause is surprising in the light of the fact(s) contained in the subordinate clause.

2. In other sentences containing concession clauses, the subordinate clause expresses something that is quite likely to be true, but which doesn't affect the truth of the main clause:

    Even if she comes top of the class, her mother will still not be satisfied.

3. In a third type of sentence the subordinate clause expresses an exception which detracts from the truth of the main clause:

    She got a good school report, although she came bottom in Biology.

Concession clauses can be introduced by the following conjunctions:

although	despite	even if	even though	except that
much as	not that	though	whereas	while/whilst

It is possible to have non-finite clauses of concession. For example:

in spite of being ill for three weeks, she still came top of the class.

Non-finite clauses of concession can be introduced by one of the following conjunctions, followed by the -ing form of the verb:

(al)though	despite	in spite of	while/whilst

It is also possible to have verbless concession clauses. These are formed by using a conjunction followed by an adjective, an adjective phrase, a prepositional phrase, or a noun phrase. For example:

*Although **unwell**, she still came top of the class.* (**ADJECTIVE**)

*Although **an invalid**, she still came top of the class.* (**NOUN PHRASE**)

The conjunctions used are:

> *(al)though   even if   if   while/whilst*

concession, adverbial of

See: **ADVERBIAL**, **ADJUNCT**

concord

See **AGREEMENT**

concrete noun

A noun which refers to anything which can be experienced using the five senses.

See also: **ABSTRACT NOUN**

condition, clause of

Conditional clauses enable us to make a variety of statements in which the truth of the main clause is dependent on the truth of the subordinate clause. There are two conjunctions used to introduce conditional clauses: 'if' and 'unless'. Conditional clauses take a variety of forms and can convey a range of meanings.

1. **Common events**
   We can use them to make statements of general truths. For example:

   > *If water freezes, it expands.*

   In sentences of this type the verbs in both the main clause and the subordinate clause are in the simple present tense.

   It is also possible to make such general statements about the past:

   > *During the 14th century if you caught the plague you died.*

2. **Possible events**
   We can make statements about hypothetical but possible events in a similar way:

   > *If her mother comes for the day her husband usually goes out.*

3. **Specific statements about the future**

A common use for conditional clauses is to speculate about possible future events. These can be 'open', in the sense that the speaker makes no assumptions about how likely the future event is:

> *If they win the next election taxes will go up.*
> *If they win the next election taxes are going to go up.*
> *If they win the next election taxes may go up.*

They can also be 'closed'. In this case the speaker indicates that the future events are to some extent unlikely:

> *If they won the next election taxes would go up.*
> *If they won the next election taxes might go up.*

4. **Hypothetical statements about the past**

It is also possible to speculate about how things might have been in the past:

> *If they had won the last election taxes would have gone up.*

This, of course, is impossible, since we now know that they didn't win the last election and so the condition remained unfulfilled.

It is also possible to construct conditional clauses without the use of a conjunction. The commonest ways of doing this are to begin the clause with 'were', 'should' , or 'had'. For example:

> *Were they to win the next election, taxes would go up.*
> *Should they win the next election, taxes would go up.*
> *Had they won the last election, taxes would have gone up.*

conjunct

The type of **ADVERBIAL** used to show a link between a sentence and one that has gone before. Examples are:

> *Moreover, in addition, meanwhile*

conjunction

Conjunctions are a class of words used to connect **WORDS**, **PHRASES**, and **CLAUSES**. If the two items to be joined are of equal grammatical

status they are joined by a **CO-ORDINATING CONJUNCTION**. In the
following examples, the co-ordinating conjunctions are printed in
bold:

> frightened **but** safe
> lemon sorbet **or** chocolate mousse
> He came **and** he conquered.

If the two items to be joined are of unequal grammatical status,
they are joined by a **SUBORDINATING CONJUNCTION**. This happens
most frequently when a **MAIN CLAUSE** and a **SUBORDINATE CLAUSE**
are combined into a **COMPLEX SENTENCE**. For example:

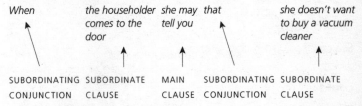

When	the householder comes to the door	she may tell you	that	she doesn't want to buy a vacuum cleaner
SUBORDINATING CONJUNCTION	SUBORDINATE CLAUSE	MAIN CLAUSE	SUBORDINATING CONJUNCTION	SUBORDINATE CLAUSE

connective

A term sometimes used to refer to **CONJUNCTS** and **DISJUNCTS**, also
known as 'sentence adverbials'.

content words

Words which 'contain' some meaning: if you look them up in a
dictionary you will find one or more definitions. They are
contrasted with structure words, which contain little or no
dictionary meaning but contribute to the structure of the
sentence. If you look these up in a dictionary you will find an
explanation of how they are used.

conversion

The process whereby a word belonging to one word class is used as
a member of another, so a noun such as 'glue' is used as a verb, for
example, or verb like 'find' is converted to a noun.

co-ordinating conjunction

A conjunction used to link two items that have the same
grammatical status. For example:

frightened **but** safe (**WORD + WORD**)

lemon sorbet **or** chocolate mousse (**PHRASE + PHRASE**)

He came **and** he conquered. (**CLAUSE + CLAUSE**)

Common co-ordinating conjunctions are:

and, but, nor, or, then, yet

co-ordination

The grammatical process by which two items of equal status are linked, using a **CO-ORDINATING CONJUNCTION**.

co-ordinator

See **CO-ORDINATING CONJUNCTION**

could

'Could' is a **MODAL AUXILIARY VERB** used to indicate possibility:

You **could** run in to them at Harlow Market.

It is also sometimes used to refer to ability:

She **could** swim well five years ago.

See also: **MAY/MIGHT**

countable noun

The majority of common nouns have singular and plural forms, because they refer to creatures or things that can be counted:

one car   several cars

a dog   his three dogs

Such nouns are described as 'countable nouns' (or sometimes 'count nouns') by contrast with 'uncountable' (or 'non-count'). A small number of countable nouns do not have a separate plural form. For example:

one sheep   two hundred sheep

dangling participle

It is quite common to begin a sentence with a construction containing a **PRESENT** or **PAST PARTICIPLE**. For example:

> ***Sitting at the window*** *Jason waited for her to arrive.*
> ***Sacked without warning*** *last week, Jason is still looking for a job.*

When you use constructions of this sort it is important to make sure that the participle refers to the **SUBJECT** of the sentence and not to some other person or thing. In the example above this has been done: the subject of the sentence is 'Jason' and 'Jason' was 'sitting at the window', and had been 'sacked without warning'. In this example, however, that has not been done:

> ***Sitting at the window*** *the car was in full view.*

What the writer appears to be saying is that the car was sitting at the window. The participle 'sitting' has been left dangling, without a subject. For the sentence to make sense, we need to provide a suitable subject and **AUXILIARY VERB**:

> <u>***While I was sitting at the window***</u> *the car was in full view.*

dare

A semi-modal verb: a verb that can be used as a modal or as a normal verb. Its normal use is similar to that of 'want':

> *She **dared** to answer back.*

It can also be used with the verb stem (without 'do' or 'to') in questions and negatives:

> ***Dare*** *I disagree?*
> *I **dare** not contradict.*

This is its modal use.

declarative clause

The type of clause used for making statements. It normally contains a **SUBJECT**, which precedes the **VERB** and which may be followed by other **CLAUSE ELEMENTS** such as an **OBJECT**, or a

COMPLEMENT. There are seven basic patterns for a declarative clause.

See also: **CLAUSE PATTERNS**

defining and non-defining relative clauses

A **RELATIVE CLAUSE** modifies the noun which lies at the centre of a noun phrase: it adds information. Sometimes that information is essential. Without it, the noun phrase no longer makes much sense because the noun headword is not sufficiently defined:

> *The people I met yesterday were incredibly boring.*

> *The people I met yesterday were incredibly boring.*

> *The people were incredibly boring.*

To say simply 'The people were incredibly boring' is not much use since it is not clear which people are referred to. Such relative clauses are described as **defining relative clauses**, since they help define the noun which they modify.

Non-defining relative clauses, on the other hand, provide additional information which does not define the noun. In the following sentence, it is quite clear to whom 'Mrs James' refers; there are unlikely to be two:

> *Mrs James is Alan's great aunt.*

So if we add a relative clause it is only for the purpose of providing additional, non-essential, information:

> *Mrs James, whom I met for the first time yesterday, is Alan's great aunt.*

Such **non-defining relative clauses** are usually enclosed between commas (or, sometimes, dashes or brackets).

deixis

See **REFERENCE**

determiner

Determiners come before a noun and help to give it some definition. Common determiners include:

all, both	a, an, the	two, three, etc
half, one-fifth, etc	this, that, these, those	second, tenth, etc
such	my, our, your, his, her, its, their	other, last, next
some, any, no	many, few, little, much	

disjunct

The type of ADVERBIAL used to make a comment or point up a contrast with what has gone before. Examples are:

by contrast, frankly

ditransitive verb

A verb that can have two ('di-') objects: a DIRECT OBJECT and AN INDIRECT OBJECT. Common ditransitive verbs include:

bring	give	offer	send
show	leave	take	get

The verbs in the following sentences are all ditransitive and the indirect objects are printed in **bold**:

*Robin Hood gave **the sheriff of Nottingham** a nasty surprise.*
*My wife bought **me** a watch.*

do

Like 'be' and 'have', 'do' can be used as either an auxiliary or as a main verb. As a main verb it has a wide range of meanings, for example:

*How are we **doing**?*
*The National Theatre are **doing** three plays by Pinter this season.*
*The new Jaguar will **do** over 110mph.*

Its main auxiliary uses are:
to make negative statements

*Camellias **don't** grow this far north.*

in forming questions

***Do** you understand this book?*

in forming TAG QUESTIONS following statements in the simple present and simple past tenses

> *The 97 goes to Greenwich, **doesn't** it?*

for emphasis

> *She **does** go on!*

to avoid repetition

> *You understand these things better than I **do**.*

This avoids having to say, 'You understand these things better than I understand these things.' See ELLIPSIS.

either/or question

A question which offers two possible responses. For example:

> *Was it Mary-Ann who left this book here, or David?*

See also: YES/NO QUESTION, QUESTION-WORD QUESTION

ellipsis

Ellipsis occurs when one or more words are omitted from a text to avoid repetition. Typically it involves replacing a complete verb phrase by an auxiliary verb. It can also involve the omission of other clause components. Common occasions for ellipsis are:

- contrasting subjects, objects, or adverbials
  *He's been there more often than I **have**.*

- use of the verbs 'to be' and 'to have'
  *The police thought he had been at the scene and he **had**.*

- use of a modal auxiliary such as *could* or *should*
  *He hasn't done as much homework as he **should**.*

Ellipsis is common in spoken English.

exclamatory clause

A type of clause used to make exclamations. Exclamatory clauses begin in one of two ways:

- *how* + ADJECTIVE

    How stupid these politicians are!

- *what* + NOUN PHRASE

    What an incredible race that was!

Exclamations can, of course, take many other forms, often as what are sometimes called 'minor' sentences:

> *Stuff and nonsense!*
> *At last!*

finite

Verbs have these forms:

> STEM: *walk, go*
> PRESENT TENSE: *walk/walks, go/goes*
> PAST TENSE: *walked, went*
> PRESENT PARTICIPLE: *walking, going*
> PAST PARTICIPLE: *walked, gone*

Of these only the present tense and the past tense are finite, or complete. The other forms require one or more AUXILIARY VERBS in order to be complete. A sentence should normally contain at least one finite verb. In the sentence that follows, the verbs are printed in italics and the finite verb in bold.

> *Walking* past the *felled* tree I ***stopped*** to *speak* to the foreman.

finite clause

A clause that contains a FINITE VERB.

focus, adverbial of

Some adverbials are used to focus attention on an element within the sentence:

> *Julian Gansworth is a famous author. He is **also** a well-known TV personality.*

Here the speaker is adding to Julian Gansworth's accomplishments, so the adverb 'also' helps focus our attention; it adds information.

Other examples of sentences with focusing adverbials are:

> *Basque, **in particular**, is a difficult language to learn.*
> ***Only** Martin Hughes failed to complete the course.*

future continuous 'tense'

This 'tense' is used to refer to a future action with emphasis on the fact that it is ongoing.

> Form: *I shall/will be working*
> Example: *Next week I shall be working over at Cranham.*

See also: TENSE

future perfect continuous 'tense'

This 'tense' is used to refer to an action that **will have been** completed at some point in the future, usually with some relevance to that particular future moment, and with emphasis on the fact that it will have been going on over a period of time.

> Form: *I shall/will have been working*
> Example: *By the end of this year I shall have been working at MFD for five years.*

See also: TENSE

future perfect 'tense'

This 'tense' refers to the past within a future period. It describes an action that **will have been** completed at some point in the future, usually with some relevance to that particular future moment.

> Form: *I shall/will have worked*
> Example: *By this evening I shall have worked out the answer.*

See also: TENSE

gerund

See VERBAL NOUN

gradable adjectives

QUALITATIVE ADJECTIVES can be **graded**: we can add to them in various ways to state more precisely how much of the quality we wish to add to the noun:

> a **beautiful** view
> a **rather beautiful** view
> an **extremely beautiful** view

and so on.

CLASSIFYING ADJECTIVES (which cannot normally be graded).

he, she, or it?

English lacks a neuter personal pronoun, so how do you avoid choosing between 'he' and 'she' in sentences like this?

> *Every writer knows that —?— should avoid sexist language.*

There are four common solutions:

1. Use 'he or she', 'him or her', and so on.
    This is an effective way of getting round the problem but can be cumbersome:

    > *Every writer knows that **he or she** should avoid sexist language.*

2. Recast the sentence so that it is in the plural.

    > *All writers know that **they** should avoid sexist language.*

    This is always acceptable, but not always possible. Some sentences do not lend themselves easily to such conversion.

3. Use the passive.

    > *Every writer knows that sexist language **should be avoided**.*

    This can be a very good solution, provided that it doesn't make the sentence too complicated or difficult to follow.

4. Use the plural pronoun as a neuter pronoun.

    > *Every writer knows that **they** should avoid sexist language.*

    This is always possible but not always acceptable, especially to traditionalists who believe that 'they' can only refer to more than one person. It is, however, widely used and increasingly accepted.

hers/*her's*

hers is a possessive pronoun, used in sentences such as:

> Sally was absolutely certain that the handbag was **hers**.
> ***her's*** does not exist.

how

A word with a number of uses:

- **as a question word**
  How are you feeling today?

- **to introduce a noun clause**
  *She won't tell me **how** they did it.*

- **to introduce an exclamatory sentence**
  How strong he looks!

I/me

Most personal pronouns have two forms, the subjective (*I, he, she, we, they*) and the objective (*me, him, her, us, them*). People sometimes get confused about whether to use 'I' or 'me'. The rule is this: use the subjective (*I*) for the subject of the sentence or clause; use the objective (*me*) for the object of the sentence or clause and after a preposition:

> My boss and **I** have been working on a new project.

but

> The Financial Controller has been helping my boss and **me.**

In very formal speech and writing, use the subjective form as the complement of the sentence:

> It is **I**.

Otherwise use the objective form:

> It is **me**.

I/one

The personal pronoun 'I' can cause problems. Sometimes people feel that they should avoid it, and it is certainly true that a text that is full of 'I' can sound rather self-important. The personal tone that the repetition of 'I' can give is also out of place in more formal writing. The solution is not, these days, to replace it with 'one'. Instead it is better to reword the text so that it is written in a more impersonal way. Instead of this:

> *I recently visited several of our customers in Zurich and I was able to tell them what I have been doing to improve the service to them.*

you can write:

> *A recent visit to several of our customers in Zurich provided an opportunity to tell them what the company is doing to improve the service to them.*

if

A subordinating conjunction used to introduce conditional clauses. For example:

> *If you don't understand that by now you must be very slow on the uptake.*

It can also be used in questions, preceded by 'What':

> *What if they decide not to come?*

This is a form of ellipsis, where the words 'what if' are a short form for 'what shall we do if', or 'what will happen if'.

imperative clause

A type of clause used to make commands and requests. Imperative clauses normally take the form of a DECLARATIVE CLAUSE in the PRESENT TENSE addressed to a second person ('you'), but with the PERSONAL PRONOUN left unstated:

> *(You) Come here!*

indirect object

Some verbs (ditransitive verbs) can have two objects: a direct object and an indirect object. This is shown in the following examples:

SUBJECT	VERB	INDIRECT OBJECT	DIRECT OBJECT
Robin Hood	*gave*	*the sheriff of Nottingham*	*a nasty surprise.*
My wife	*bought*	*me*	*a watch.*

Each type of object is affected in a different way by the action referred to in the verb: the indirect object receives or benefits from the direct object.

infinitive

The form of the verb used in a **VERB PHRASE** after verbs like 'want', 'help', and 'let':

> *She said she wanted **to go** home.*
> *My father helped me **pack**.*

As can be seen from these examples, there are two forms of the infinitive:

- the verb stem: 'pack'
- the verb stem preceded by 'to': 'to go'

The 'to' infinitive is also used in expressions such as:

> *To err is human, to forgive divine.*

Here it functions like a **NOUN** or **NOUN PHRASE**. Used in this way it can, for example, serve as the **SUBJECT**, **OBJECT**, or **COMPLEMENT** of the **CLAUSE**.

See also: **SPLIT INFINITIVE**

infinitive clause

A **CLAUSE** which contains no **FINITE** verb, but has the verb **STEM** preceded by 'to'. For example:

> *They will decide **when to stop the action**.*
> *I deliberately slowed my pace **so as to look tired**.*

inflection

Some **NOUNS**, **VERBS**, and **ADJECTIVES** change their form according to usage. This change of form is called **inflection**. Nouns inflect to show plural:

> one car—several car**s**
> one woman—several wom**en**

Verbs inflect to show **NUMBER** and **PERSON** in the **PRESENT TENSE**, to show the **PAST TENSE**, the **PRESENT** and **PAST PARTICIPLES**:

> I work—she work**s** (present tense)
> I work—I work**ed** (past tense)
> work—work**ing** (present participle)—work**ed** (past participle)

Some adjectives inflect to show comparison:

> big—big**ger**—big**gest**

intensifier

An adverb that is used to **MODIFY** an adjective. Intensifiers have the effect of changing the amount of a quality something has. For example, compare the different meanings of these:

> an easy victory
> a **fairly** easy victory
> an **incredibly** easy victory

Intensifying adverbs can also modify other adverbs. For example:

> easily
> **fairly easily**
> **incredibly** easily

interrogative clause

An interrogative clause is used to ask questions. It differs from a **DECLARATORY CLAUSE** in that the form of the **VERB** is changed and often part of it comes before the **SUBJECT**:

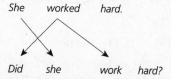

VERB   SUBJECT   VERB   REST OF SENTENCE

This inversion of subject and verb does not, however, occur in **QUESTION-WORD QUESTIONS** (see below):

She   *worked*   *hard.*

↓   ↓   ↓

Who   *worked*   *hard?*

There are three forms of question:

- **yes/no questions**
- **question-word questions**
- **either/or questions**

intransitive verb

Main verbs can be divided into **TRANSITIVE, INTRANSITIVE,** and **LINKING.** Intransitive verbs are those which do not require an **OBJECT.**

> Examples: groan, laugh
> Sample sentence: *The injured man was groaning.*

Some verbs can be both transitive and intransitive.

> Examples: paint, dream

Sample sentences:

> *The master was painting.*
> *He painted several abstracts.*

irregular verb

Irregular verbs are those which do not form their past tense and past participle from the stem in a regular way, as 'work' does, for example:

STEM	PAST TENSE	PAST PARTICIPLE
work	worked	worked

Examples of irregular verbs are 'drive', 'lay', and 'burst':

STEM	PAST TENSE	PAST PARTICIPLE
drive	drove	driven
lay	lay	laid
burst	burst	burst

As can be seen from these examples, not all irregular verbs are irregular in the same way. Two are completely different from all the others:

STEM	PAST TENSE	PAST PARTICIPLE
be	was/were	been
go	went	gone

Each of these two verbs derives from two different Old English verbs, which accounts for their unusual patterns. Other irregular verbs vary considerably:

STEM	PAST TENSE	PAST PARTICIPLE
make	made	made
swell	swelled	swollen
say	said	said
blow	blew	blown
fight	fought	fought
swim	swam	swum

is/are

Verbs have different forms in the SIMPLE PRESENT TENSE according to the NUMBER and PERSON of the SUBJECT. In the verb 'be' these are:

	SINGULAR	PLURAL
1ST PERSON	I am	we are
2ND PERSON	you are (thou art)	you are
3RD PERSON	he/she/it is	they are

This verb also has different forms in the simple past tense:

	SINGULAR	PLURAL
1ST PERSON	I was	we were
2ND PERSON	you were (thou wert)	you were
3RD PERSON	he/she/it was	they were

If the subject is a single word, or a short **NOUN PHRASE**, there is usually little difficulty in ensuring that the verb agrees with the subject. But if the subject is an extended noun phrase, it is possible to lose track of the number of the subject. For example:

> *The new catalogue, which included the IX34 autocleaner, the TR43 tray insert, the B7 grommit clip, and the new range of fascia accessories,* ***were*** *described as innovative and exciting.*

The subject of this sentence is a noun phrase which can be broken down in this way:

DETERMINER	PREMODIFIER	HEADWORD	POSTMODIFIER
The	*new*	*catalogue*	*which included… autocleaner*

The verb must agree with the **headword** 'catalogue' and should, therefore, be 'was'.

It + passive

A common usage is to begin a sentence with it, followed by a passive. For example:

> ***It*** *is felt that your actions were inappropriate.*

Here the writer is trying to avoid responsibility, by refusing to use the active and give the verb a subject. (Compare: 'I think you behaved badly.') Such usage is mealy-mouthed.

On the other hand, the construction may be quite useful:

> **It** is believed that production figures for the third quarter are well down.

The writer may well not have a clear idea of exactly whose opinion is being quoted, although it is quite clear that the belief is widespread. In such a case the use of *It* + passive is useful.

its/it's

its = of it
it's = it is

> This book has lost **its** cover.
> **It's** because people don't look after library books.

just

This adverb has two different meanings:

1. 'a short time ago':
   *They have **just** arrived.*
   (In this sense, in British English 'just' is used with a perfect tense.)

2. 'only':
   *I **just** had time to get back onto the pavement.*

Confusion can sometimes occur in sentences such as this:

> *I have **just** bought a newspaper.*

This could mean either 'I bought a newspaper a short time ago,' or 'I only bought a newspaper.' In spoken English the ambiguity can usually be overcome by stress and intonation, but in written English it may be necessary to rephrase the sentence to remove the ambiguity.

lexis

The store of words a language contains, often called its vocabulary. The term 'lexis' is used to refer to the word level of language:

> **WORDS** contribute to **PHRASES**, which form **CLAUSES**, which build into **SENTENCES**.

like/as

'Like' is used as a conjunction in sentences such as:

*He looks **like** his father.*

In informal usage it is also frequently used as a conjunction:

*He looks **like** he needs a holiday.*

This is, however, frowned on by many purists and it is advisable to avoid using 'like' as a conjunction if you wish to avoid being considered 'uneducated' (despite the fact that this usage dates back at least as far as Shakespeare). Instead of 'like', use 'as' or 'as if':

*He looks **as if** he needs a holiday.*

linking verb

Main verbs can be divided into TRANSITIVE, INTRANSITIVE and LINKING verbs, according to the ways in which they are used in a CLAUSE. Linking verbs are used in clauses of this pattern:

SUBJECT	VERB	COMPLEMENT
Peter and Liz	are	singers.
She	seems	sad.

By far the commonest linking verb is 'be'. Others are: 'seem', 'appear', 'become', and 'look'. Note, however, that some of these can also be used as intransitive verbs. For example:

*Then a ghost **appeared**. It looked straight through me.*

main clause

Every sentence contains a main clause. If you join two main clauses together using *and, but* or other CO-ORDINATING CONJUNCTIONS you make a compound sentence.

ONE MAIN CLAUSE: *The stock market collapsed.*
ONE MAIN CLAUSE: *Jemma lost all her money.*
TWO MAIN CLAUSES: *The stock market collapsed and Jemma lost all her money.*

It is possible to join these two clauses in other ways: by making one of them the main clause and the other a less important, or subordinate, clause:

> *When the stock market collapsed,*   *Jemma lost all her money.*
>   MAIN CLAUSE
>
> *The stock market collapsed*   *after Jemma lost all her money.*
> MAIN CLAUSE

main verb

The VERB PHRASE in a CLAUSE can contain two types of verb: MAIN VERBS and AUXILIARY VERBS. It may or may not contain one or more auxiliary verbs, but it **must** contain a main verb. In these SIMPLE (one clause) SENTENCES the main verb is printed in bold type:

> *Yesterday I **received** a large bill.*
> *It **was** from an internet service provider.*
> *I have been **using** the internet a lot recently.*

See also: PRIMARY VERB

manner, adverbial of

A common use of adverbials is to give information about **how** events occur. In the following sample sentences, the adverbials are printed in bold:

> *The raft drifted **slowly** towards the rocks.*
> *She did her shopping **at great speed**.*

See also: ADVERBIAL, ADJUNCT

manner, clause of

Adverbial clauses of manner answer the question 'How?'. They provide information about how the action described in the main clause was performed:

> *Mrs Smith complained as she always does.*

We can also compare an action or a state with something else:

> *He ran as if his life depended on it.*

Conjunctions used to introduce clauses of manner are:

as   *as if*   *as though*
just as   *much as*

Non-finite clauses of manner can be introduced by 'as if' and 'as though'. These are then followed by 'to' plus the verb stem:

*She shook her head vigorously **as if to** get rid of unwelcome thoughts.*

may

'May' is a **MODAL AUXILIARY VERB** used to indicate:

- **permission**: *You **may** leave if you wish.*

- **possibility**: *They **may** come over tomorrow.*

See also: **CAN/MAY, MAY/MIGHT**

may/might

These two **MODAL AUXILIARY VERBS** are sometimes confused. They refer to situations which are possible:

1. *They **may** contact us next week.*

2. *They **might** contact us next week.*

3. *They **may** have contacted us last week.*

4. *They **might** have contacted us last week.*

Sentences 1 and 2 refer to possible future events. Sentence 1 describes a situation that is completely open: they may contact us or they may not. In sentence 2 the situation is viewed as somewhat less likely: they may contact us, but on balance they probably won't. Sentences 3 and 4 work in a similar way but refer to a past event.

   Sometimes might is used to refer to a situation that was possible once, but now is not:

*If their computers hadn't been down, they **might** have contacted us.*

It would be confusing to use 'may' instead of 'might' in such a sentence, since it implies that the situation described is possible and open, when in fact it is impossible and closed.

might

'Might' is a **MODAL AUXILIARY VERB** used to indicate possibility:

> That **might** well be the best thing to do.

See also: **MAY/MIGHT**

modal auxiliary

Auxiliary verbs work with the **MAIN VERB** in a **CLAUSE** to form the **VERB PHRASE**. The modal auxiliaries are:

> shall/will/should/would
> can/could
> may/might
> must
> ought (to)

Whereas **PRIMARY AUXILIARIES** are used to refer to actual events in the past or the present, modal auxiliaries are used to refer to possible events. They express varying degrees of possibility, as is illustrated by these examples:

> They **will** spend next week in New York.
> They **could** spend next week in New York.
> They **might** spend next week in New York.

In each case the verb indicates the speaker's opinion about the possible event—and the likelihood of its actually occurring. Modal auxiliaries can also be used to show how **desirable** an event is:

> They **ought to** spend next week in New York.
> They **must** spend next week in New York.

modifier

A word or group of words that modifies another word is called a modifier. For example, in the following noun phrase, the modifiers are printed in **bold**.

> the **last** Christmas **of the old millennium**

Modifiers that come before the word they modify are referred to as **premodifiers**; those that come after are **postmodifiers**.
See also: **NOUN PHRASE**

modify

A word or group of words that affects the meaning of another word is said to modify it. In each of the phrases that follow, the modifiers are printed in bold.

> ADJECTIVE PHRASE: **rather** large
> ADVERB PHRASE: **very** elegantly
> NOUN PHRASE: **beautiful** clothes

morpheme

The lowest unit of language that can convey meaning. You cannot break a morpheme down into anything smaller that means anything. Many simple words are morphemes, for example:

> child   toy   play

Sometimes, however, a word consists of two or more morphemes:

> child + ren   toy + s   play + ing

-ren, -s, and -ing all convey meaning, although they are not words and cannot stand alone. If we try to break these morphemes down any more, we are left with sounds or letters:

> r + e + n

None of these conveys any meaning on its own. The study of how morphemes work is called MORPHOLOGY.

morphology

The study of MORPHEMES: the forms of words and parts of words.

multiple sentence

A sentence consisting of two or more CLAUSES.

must

'Must' is a MODAL AUXILIARY VERB. It expresses the speaker's view of how desirable a possible event is:

> I **must** go home now.

need

A semi-modal verb: a verb that can be used as a modal or as a normal verb. Its normal use is:

- as a transitive verb:
  They **needed** a break.

- with 'to' plus the verb stem (similar to 'want'):
  They **needed** to rest for a while.

It can also be used with the verb stem (without 'do' or 'to') in questions and negatives:

> **Need I say more?**
> I **need** not continue.

This is its modal use.

nominal clause

See NOUN CLAUSE

non-defining relative clause

See DEFINING AND NON-DEFINING RELATIVE CLAUSES

none are/none is

Some traditionalists say that the pronoun none should always be followed by a singular verb: none is is always right and none are is always wrong. They argue that none comes from no one and so is always singular. This is mistaken. Using none to mean no persons is now commoner than using it to mean no one. If you wish to make it clear that there was only one individual involved, then you have to say no one.

In general, none is best followed by the form of the verb which makes best sense, as in the following examples:

> I have met several famous writers, but none **is** more approachable than Jerry Spriggs.
> I have interviewed a lot of journalists, too, but none **are** as interesting as Jerry.

non-finite clause

A clause that does not contain a FINITE verb, but has, instead, the word 'to' plus the verb STEM (the infinitive), the PRESENT PARTICIPLE, or the PAST PARTICIPLE. For example:

> *They will decide **when to stop the action**.*
> *I realised the truth **while reading through the trial documents**.*
> *The story began with words **taken from the Bible**.*

nor

A CO-ORDINATING CONJUNCTION, often used as part of a pair: *neither…nor*.

noun

A class of words used to refer to people, things, and ideas. Most nouns satisfy all or most of the following tests:

> they can be preceded by *a, an,* or *the*
> *a **pen**, an **answer**, the **train***

they have a singular and a plural form:

> *one **pen**, two **pens***

they can form the headword of a noun phrase:

> *the blue **pen** on the table*

they can be preceded by an adjective:

> *blue **pens**, interesting **answers***

Nouns fall into a number of different groupings, which can be illustrated by this simple diagram:

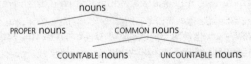

noun clause

A subordinate clause that can act as the subject, object, subject complement, or object complement of a complex sentence. For example:

> ***What I want to do now*** *is have five minutes' rest.* (**SUBJECT**)
> *The letter explained* ***how the accident happened***. (**OBJECT**)
> *The problem is* ***when we should go***. (**SUBJECT COMPLEMENT**)
> *His loving mother made him* ***what he is today***. (**OBJECT**
> **COMPLEMENT**)

Noun clauses can be introduced by: *that, what, why, when, where, how, whether, if.*

noun phrase

A group of words built up round a single noun, the headword of the phrase. In the following noun phrases the headword is printed in bold:

> *some **books***
> *some interesting **books***
> *some interesting **books** about South America*

Noun phrases can consist of these parts:

DETERMINER	PREMODIFIER	HEADWORD	POSTMODIFIER
some	*interesting*	*books*	*about South America*

In sentences, noun phrases can be:

- the subject of a clause

- the object of a clause

- the subject complement of a clause

- the object complement of a clause

- part of a larger phrase, for example a prepositional phrase

number

The subject of a clause can be singular (consisting of one creature, thing, or idea) or plural (consisting of more than one). Most nouns have singular and plural forms, as do pronouns. The present tense form of verbs has corresponding singular and plural forms and subject and verb should agree in number.

The variations caused by number and person are shown most obviously in the verb 'be':

	SINGULAR	PLURAL
1ST PERSON	I am	we are
2ND PERSON	you are (thou art)	you are
3RD PERSON	he/she/it is	they are

In other verbs, however, there are only two forms: the verb stem and the verb stem plus 's':

	SINGULAR	PLURAL
1ST PERSON	I walk	we walk
2ND PERSON	you walk	you walk
3RD PERSON	he/she/it walks	they walk

The only verb to have different forms in the simple past tense is 'be':

	SINGULAR	PLURAL
1ST PERSON	I was	we were
2ND PERSON	you were	you were
3RD PERSON	he/she/it was	they were

See also: AGREEMENT

object

The object of a statement clause normally comes after the verb and refers to a different person or thing from the subject. The object can be:

■ a noun

■ a pronoun

■ a noun phrase

In the following sentences the objects are printed in **bold**:

> Anita just lost **her airline ticket and her passport**.
> An airport official found **them**.

object complement

Part of a clause that completes the meaning of the object. In a statement clause it comes after the object and refers to the same person, thing, or idea as the object. Examples:

SUBJECT	VERB	OBJECT	OBJECT COMPLEMENT
The directors	made	Edith Saunders	their new Chair.
This	made	her	very pleased.

The object complement can be:

- a noun
  *They made me **Secretary**.*

- a noun phrase
  *They made me **Chairman of the Finance Committee**.*

- an adjective or adjective phrase
  *They made me **angry**.*

objective case

See CASE

or

A **CO-ORDINATING CONJUNCTION**, often used as part of a pair: *either…or.*

ought to

'Ought to' is a **MODAL AUXILIARY VERB** used to refer to possible rather than actual events. It expresses the speaker's view of the event's desirability. For example:

> *I **ought to** go home now.*

paragraph

Written texts that consist of more than a few sentences are, by convention, divided into paragraphs. These are units each consisting of a relatively small number of sentences focusing on an aspect of the topic of the text. Either the first sentence or, occasionally, the second or third sentence of the paragraph is a topic sentence, which introduces the subject matter of the paragraph. Succeeding sentences develop the topic and there is frequently a concluding sentence which rounds off the paragraph and, often, leads into the following paragraph.

passive voice

Transitive verbs can be used in two different ways or 'voices'; active and passive:

> ACTIVE: *A speeding car **struck** our house.*
> PASSIVE: *Our house **was struck** by a speeding car.*

In the passive voice, it is as if the object of the sentence suddenly gets a voice of its own and can describe an event from its own point of view. As can be seen from the example above, this applies even when it is inanimate.

The transformation from active to passive works like this:

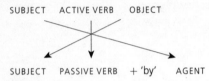

For example:

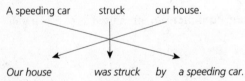

All 'tenses' can occur in the passive voice, but some are fairly uncommon:

	SIMPLE	CONTINUOUS	PERFECT	PERFECT CONTINUOUS
PAST	I was struck	I was being struck	I had been struck	I had been being struck
PRESENT	I am struck	I am being struck	I have been struck	I have been being struck
FUTURE	I shall be struck	I shall be being struck	I shall have been struck	I shall have been being struck

See also: **ACTIVE VOICE**

passive voice—usage

Advocates of 'plain English' urge that writers should avoid the passive voice. It certainly has a number of disadvantages, of which the main two are:

1. It tends to sound rather formal and remote:
   This bin should not be used for confidential waste paper.

2. It can lead to unnecessarily convoluted expressions:
   New excavations of the site were begun by a team of archaeologists led by Professor Dunbar.

Sentence 1 would be better and simpler as:

> *Do not throw confidential papers in this bin.*

Sentence 2 would begin to become simpler if it were made active:

> *Professor Dunbar led a team that started to excavate the site.*

Sometimes, however, it is useful to avoid the more personal touch of the active voice and to use the more impersonal passive voice:

> *Unfortunately your brother was run over by a speeding car.*

Many would find this preferable to:

> *Unfortunately a speeding car ran your brother over.*

which is more direct, but also more brutal.

See also: *It* + passive

past continuous 'tense'

This 'tense' is used to refer to an action in the past with emphasis that it went on over a period of time.

> Form: *I was reading*
> Example: *She was reading a book.*

The past continuous is often used to contrast with the **SIMPLE PAST**:

> *He phoned while she was reading a book.*

SIMPLE PAST   PAST CONTINUOUS

See also: **TENSE**

past participle

One of the **FORMS OF THE VERB**. In regular verbs the past participle is formed by adding '-ed' or '-d' to the verb **STEM**. In **IRREGULAR VERBS** it is formed in a variety of ways. It is used to form the following '**TENSES**' in the **ACTIVE VOICE**:

> PRESENT PERFECT: *I have walked*
> PAST PERFECT: *I had walked*
> FUTURE PERFECT: *I shall have walked*

It is also used to form the **PASSIVE VOICE** tenses.

past perfect continuous 'tense'

This 'tense' is used to refer to a continuing action in the past contrasted with a single completed action in the past (in the **SIMPLE PAST 'TENSE'**).

> Form: *I had been walking*
> Example: *After I had been walking for some time, I stopped for a rest.*

past perfect continuous   simple past

See also: **TENSE**

past perfect 'tense'

This 'tense' is used to refer to a completed action in the past, usually contrasted with one which came after it (in the **SIMPLE PAST**).

> Form: *I had finished*
> Example: *When they had finished their coffee, they paid the bill.*

past perfect   simple past

See also: **TENSE**

past tense

One of the two **FORMS OF THE VERB** which modern grammar

recognises as a true TENSE, the other being the PRESENT TENSE. In regular verbs it is formed by adding '-ed' to the verb STEM and is thus identical in form to the PAST PARTICIPLE. It is used to refer to a single completed action in the past, or to an action that continued over a period, or to a series of completed past actions:

> *They ran away.*
> *That week he worked on the account every evening.*
> *She telephoned her brother every Tuesday morning.*

See also: SIMPLE PAST, TENSE

perfect aspect

The perfect (or perfective) aspect of the VERB PHRASE is formed by using the PAST PARTICIPLE of the MAIN VERB and preceding it by one or more AUXILIARY VERBS which always include either 'have' or 'had':

> PRESENT PERFECT: *I have walked*
> PAST PERFECT: *I had walked*
> FUTURE PERFECT: *I shall have walked*

The perfect aspect is used to refer to a completed action that is still relevant to the moment the speaker is referring to (present, past, or future) and/or is still affecting that moment in some way. So, for example, if someone says, 'I have lived in Wandsworth for ten years,' it means that they are still living there as they speak. If, by contrast, they say, 'I lived in Wandsworth for ten years,' they mean that they no longer live there.

The perfect aspect can also be combined with the CONTINUOUS ASPECT:

> PRESENT PERFECT CONTINUOUS: *I have been walking*
> PAST PERFECT CONTINUOUS: *I had been walking*
> FUTURE PERFECT CONTINUOUS: *I shall have been walking*

Here the action referred to is regarded as complete (at least, for the moment) and relevant to the moment referred to, but there is additional emphasis on the period of time over which the action continued. Compare these two sentences:

> *I had walked six miles before I found her.*
> *I had been walking for two hours before I found her.*

person

PERSONAL PRONOUNS can be 1st, 2nd, or 3rd person. The 1st person refers either to the speaker or to a group which includes the speaker: 'I' and 'we'. The 2nd person refers to the person(s) the speaker is addressing: 'you'. The 3rd person refers to any other people or things: 'he', 'she', 'it', and 'they'.

See also: **AGREEMENT**, **NUMBER**

phrasal verbs

A phrasal verb is made up of a verb plus an adverb. Phrasal verbs can be intransitive or transitive. For example:

INTRANSITIVE	TRANSITIVE
back away	carry out
catch on	dig up
hold on	leave behind
settle down	spell out

The adverb in transitive phrasal verbs can often come either before or after the object:

The dog dug up the bone.
The dog dug the bone up.

If the object is a personal preposition, then it usually precedes the adverb:

They left me behind.

If the object is an extended noun phrase it is usually more convenient to place it after the adverb:

She spelled out the difficulties involved in moving house.

phrase

A group of words based on a headword. There are five types of phrase in English:

■ **NOUN PHRASE**

- **VERB PHRASE**

- **PREPOSITIONAL PHRASE**

- **ADJECTIVE PHRASE**

- **ADVERB PHRASE**

Phrases are combined to form CLAUSES.

place, adverbial of

A common use of adverbials is to give information about **where** events occur. In the following sample sentences, the adverbials are printed in bold:

> *I didn't expect to see you **here**.*
> *The match was played **at the Oval**.*
> ***Down in Somerset** the roads have been very busy this weekend.*

See also: ADVERBIAL, ADJUNCT

place, clause of

Adverbial clauses of place answer the question, 'Where?'. They give information about the place where the event in the main clause occurred:

> *She hid the treasure where no one could find it.*

Conjunctions used to introduce adverbial clauses of place are:

> *where   wherever   everywhere*

plural

See NUMBER

possessive case

See CASE

possessive determiner

The following words are known as possessive determiners:

my	our
your	
his	their
her	
its	

They come before a noun in a noun phrase. For example:

> *my* mother
> *our* black and white cocker spaniel

They are sometimes described as 'possessive pronouns' (see below) or 'possessive adjectives', but both these terms are misleading.

possessive pronoun

The following words are described as possessive pronouns:

mine	ours
yours	
his	theirs
hers	
its	

These pronouns show possession and act as pronouns because they can stand on their own as the subject, object, or complement of a clause:

> This scarf is *yours*. (**COMPLEMENT**)
> *Mine* is on the table. (**SUBJECT**)
> Miriam lost *hers* a long time ago. (**OBJECT**)

postmodifier

See **MODIFIER**

predicative adjective

Most adjectives can form the complement of a sentence. For example:

*That novel is **terrible!***
*Her unpunctuality used to make me **irritable**.*

This use of adjectives is known as predicative. It contrasts with the attributive use of adjectives, when they modify a noun. A small number of adjectives can only be used predicatively, for example 'alone'.

prefix

Part of a word that comes before the BASE. In the words that follow the prefixes are printed in bold:

autobiography, **super**market, **dis**interested

Prefixes add to or alter the meaning of the base word in some way. For examples of prefix meanings, see **mega-**, **self-**, and **trans-** in this section.

premodifier

See MODIFIER

preposition

Prepositions are words that are placed before a NOUN, PRONOUN, VERBAL NOUN or NOUN PHRASE to form a PREPOSITIONAL PHRASE:

with marbles (noun)
to me (pronoun)
for walking (verbal noun)
down a long dusty road (noun phrase)

The commonest are:

about	above	across	after	against	along
among	around	as	at	before	behind
below	beneath	beside	between	beyond	but
by	despite	during	except	for	from
in	inside	into	less	like	near
of	off	on	over	past	round
since	through	throughout	till	to	towards
under	underneath	until	up	upon	with
within	without				

preposition at end of sentence

There are still people who say that you should never end a sentence with a preposition. They argue that since the term 'preposition' describes a word that is positioned **before** ('pre-') another word, it is wrong to place it at the end of a sentence where it cannot come before anything. In fact it is sometimes necessary to put a preposition at the end, since there is no other way of constructing the sentence.

The alternative didn't bear thinking about.

Sometimes it is possible to reword a sentence to avoid putting a preposition at the end. This sentence:

This is the book you asked for.

can be recast as:

This is the book for which you asked.

The alternative version, however, is much more formal, and many would find it a little pompous. In fact, it is only in academic texts that writers try to avoid placing a preposition at the end of a sentence. In most other writing, this is a 'rule' that you can happily ignore.

prepositional phrase

A group of words consisting of a **PREPOSITION** (which always comes at the beginning) followed by a **NOUN**, **VERBAL NOUN**, **PRONOUN**, or **NOUN PHRASE**. Prepositional phrases are commonly used:

- **to modify a noun**
  *a new book **by James Rees***

  In this case they usually come after the noun (they **postmodify** it).

- **as an ADVERBIAL**
  *She put the book **on the table**.*

prepositional verbs

These consist of a verb followed by a preposition. For example:

decide on   lead to   rely on

It may seem difficult to distinguish between PHRASAL VERBS and
prepositional verbs, since some words can be both prepositions and
adverbs (for example 'off'). The distinction is that the preposition of
a prepositional verb must be followed by a noun, pronoun, or noun
phrase. So all prepositional verbs are transitive. In addition, the
object must come after the preposition. So while it is correct to say:

> *She decided on the blue skirt.*

you cannot say:

> *She decided the blue skirt on.*

present continuous 'tense'

The CONTINUOUS ASPECT of the present 'tense'. This 'tense' is used for
a number of different purposes. The commonest are listed below.
Form: *I am walking*

1. **actions going on now**
   I'm calling from the station.

2. **actions continuing over a period including the present**
   We're staying with the Bentons this week.

3. **actions planned for the future**
   I'm going to a conference in Brussels next week.

See also: SIMPLE PRESENT 'TENSE', TENSE

present participle

One of the forms of the verb. It is formed by adding '-ing' to the
verb stem. It is used to make continuous 'tenses' by adding one or
more auxiliary verbs before it:

> VERB: *walk*
> PRESENT PARTICIPLE: *walking*
> PRESENT CONTINUOUS: *I am walking*
> PAST CONTINUOUS: *I was walking*

and so on.

The present participle is also used to form non-finite clauses. These are similar in form and general meaning to finite clauses but they lack a finite auxiliary. Often, too, the subject is omitted and understood:

> *Those two men **walking up the hill** look a bit suspicious to me.*

The words 'walking up the hill' are like a short form of '**who are** walking up the hill'. A non-finite clause containing a present participle can also be used at the beginning of a sentence:

> ***Walking up the hill**, he noticed two suspicious-looking men in a doorway.*

Here the words 'Walking up the hill' are a short form of '**As he was** walking up the hill'.

present perfect continuous 'tense'

This 'tense' is used to refer to a completed past action with results lasting into the present, but with an emphasis on the fact that the action went on over a period of time.

> Form: *I have been working*
> Example: *I have been working in Reading this week.*

See also: TENSE

present perfect 'tense'

This 'tense' is used to refer to a completed past action with results lasting into the present.

> Form: *I have written*
> Example: *I have written fifteen letters today.*

It is also used to refer to a series of completed past actions with results lasting into the present. For example: *She's telephoned me every day this week!*

See also: TENSE

present tense

One of the two FORMS OF THE VERB which modern grammar recognises as a true TENSE, the other being the PAST TENSE. It is the same as the verb STEM, or is formed by adding '-s' to the verb stem:

	SINGULAR	PLURAL
1ST PERSON	I walk	we walk
2ND PERSON	you walk	you walk
3RD PERSON	he/she/it walks	they walk

See also: SIMPLE PRESENT (for an explanation of its uses) and TENSE

primary auxiliary verbs

These are the verbs 'be' and 'have'. They have a dual function. They work as auxiliaries:

> It **is** raining.
> The rain **has** just stopped.

They can also stand on their own as main verbs in the sentence:

> The weather **is** rather disappointing.
> Fortunately I **have** an umbrella.

Primary auxiliary verbs are used to form a number of 'tenses' of the verb phrase:

> PRESENT CONTINUOUS: I **am** walking
> PRESENT PERFECT: I **have** walked
> PRESENT PERFECT CONTINUOUS: I **have been** walking

and so on.

pronoun

Pronouns are a class of words that 'stand in for' other words, typically for nouns, noun phrases, and other pronouns. They enable the writer or speaker to refer to a word, expression, or idea that has already been mentioned, without having to repeat it. In this sample paragraph the pronouns are printed in bold type. The number beside each one links it to the explanation that follows.

I (1) *had an unfortunate accident last week. I* (2) *was walking out of the office when I* (3) *slipped on the floor.* **It** (4) *was wet because the cleaners had just been through and* **they** (5) *hadn't mopped it* (6) *dry.* **It** (7) *wasn't the first time that* **this** (8) *had happened,* **which** (9) *was very irritating.*

1, 2, and 3. 'I' refers to the writer.

4. 'It' refers to 'the floor'

5. 'they' refers to 'the cleaners'

6. 'it' refers to 'the floor'

7. 'It' doesn't refer back to anything at all. It is called a 'dummy subject'—it is a useful way of constructing that kind of sentence.

8. 'this' refers to the whole event: the cleaner's failing to mop the floor properly and someone slipping on it.

9. 'which' refers to 'It wasn't the first time that this had happened'.

Pronouns have many uses and so it is not surprising that there are several different groups, which are formed and used in different ways:

Personal	I/me, we/us, you, he/him, she/her, it, they/them
Possessive	mine, ours, yours, his, hers, its, theirs
Reflexive	myself, ourselves, yourself, yourselves, himself, herself, itself, themselves
Demonstrative	this, that, these, those
Indefinite	some, someone, somebody, something any, anyone, anybody, anything none, no one, nobody, nothing everyone, everybody, everything, all either, neither, both, each
Interrogative	who, whom, whose, what, which
Relative	who, whom, whose, which, that

See also: **PERSONAL PRONOUN, POSSESSIVE PRONOUN, REFLEXIVE PRONOUN, DEMONSTRATIVE PRONOUN, INDEFINITE PRONOUN, INTERROGATIVE PRONOUN, RELATIVE PRONOUN**

proper noun

Proper nouns are a group of words that refer to people, places, or things that are unique. In written English they are spelt with an initial capital letter:

Ethiopia   George

(You might reasonably object that there is more than one 'George' in the world, but within any English sentence when we use the word 'George' it refers to a person who is unique in the text.) Proper nouns can also consist of more than one word:

The Merry Wives of Windsor   King Charles III

purpose, clause of

Clauses of purpose answer the question 'Why?'. They explain events or states in the main clause by referring to the intentions of one or more participants:

I turned the car round so that I could make a quick getaway.

Non-finite clauses of purpose are often simpler to use than finite ones and are frequently preferred. They are introduced by 'to', or by a conjunction ending with 'to' followed by the verb stem:

I turned the car round so as to make a quick getaway.

The conjunctions used vary according to whether the clause is finite or non-finite:

FINITE	NON-FINITE
in order that	*in order to*
so that	*so as to*
so	*to*

qualitative adjective

adjectives fall into two broad groups: CLASSIFYING adjectives, which place the noun they modify into a category, and qualitative adjectives. As the name suggests, the latter attribute qualities to the creature, thing, or idea to which the noun refers:

*A **large green** automobile*

Qualitative adjectives can have COMPARATIVE and SUPERLATIVE forms and can be GRADED.

question-word question

A question that expects an answer containing information. Question-word questions begin with these words:

who(m), which, what, when, where, why, how

For example:

Why did you leave her?

Because of the form of the question words, these questions are sometimes called 'WH-QUESTIONS'.

quite

The adverb 'quite' has a range of uses of which a very common one is as a MODIFIER used before an adjective or adverb:

That is quite impossible.
She moved forward quite slowly.

It has two meanings, however:

- 'completely'
  quite impossible

- 'fairly'
  quite slowly

If 'quite' modifies an adjective or adverb that can be graded, the second meaning is usually intended, as in the example above. Otherwise it is the first. This is not always true, however, and confusion can arise:

Their garden is quite beautiful.

Does the speaker mean 'fairly' or 'completely' here? (Or is the statement deliberately ambiguous?)

reason, adverbial of

See also: ADVERBIAL, ADJUNCT

reason, clause of

Adverbial clauses of reason answer the question, 'Why?'. They give an explanation of why the event or state described in the main clause occurred:

> *The plan was unsuccessful because they hadn't thought it through.*
> *Since the scheme needed a lot of money it never got off the ground.*

The main conjunctions used to introduce clauses of reason are:

> *as   because   since*

reference

Since the reading of a written text is essentially a linear experience, taking place in what we now call 'real time', referring back to ideas, sentences, phrases, and words that have gone before is a key way for writers to 'take their readers with them' and give their texts COHESION. Referring forwards, telling readers what is about to happen in the text, also enables them to keep some control of the reading process. Referring backwards is sometimes called ANAPHORIC reference, while referring forwards is CATAPHORIC reference.

The main grammatical means used to refer forwards and back are:

- **REFERRING WORDS**
  Words like pronouns, which enable us to refer clearly and briefly to what has gone before, or what is coming later, without repetition.

- **ELLIPSIS**
  Constructions that enable us to refer back to earlier material, while missing out sections of sentences without confusing the reader or listener.

- **CONJUNCTS** and **DISJUNCTS**
  These can make clear the links between sentences in the text.

Reference is also known as **DEIXIS**.

referring words

We can refer backwards and forwards in a text by using:

- **personal pronouns**
  she, they etc

- **demonstrative pronouns**
  this, that, these, those

- **relative pronouns**
  which

- **determiners**
  the, three etc

- **other words and phrases**
  former, latter, above, below etc
  argument, opinion, notion etc

regular verb

Regular verbs make their past tense and past participle by adding '-ed' or '-d' to the verb stem:

> *walk → walked*
> *rinse → rinsed*

This is in contrast to **IRREGULAR VERBS**, which do not follow this pattern.

relative clause

Relative clauses are used as postmodifiers in a noun phrase and do a similar job to adjectives:

> He was an **obese** man. *(adjective)*
> He was a man **who clearly had a weight problem**. *(relative clause)*

In their full form, relative clauses are like mini-sentences. You can remove them from the sentence they are in and with very few changes turn them into sentences in their own right:

ORIGINAL	BECOMES
*He was a man **who clearly** **had a weight problem***.	*He was a man. **He clearly** **had a weight problem***.

It is also possible to postmodify a noun with a non-finite clause. These clauses work in much the same way as relative clauses and fulfil a similar purpose:

VERB FORM	SAMPLE SENTENCE	EQUIVALENT USING FULL RELATIVE CLAUSE
INFINITIVE	*That's not the approach **to take** with her*.	*That's not the approach **that you should take** with her*.
PRESENT PARTICIPLE	*That's the man **taking** all the pictures of us*.	*That's the man **who has been taking** all the pictures of us*.
PAST PARTICIPLE	*This is a picture **taken** last week*.	*This is a picture **that was taken** last week*.

Relative clauses can be **DEFINING** or **NON-DEFINING**.

repetition

The repetition of words, phrases, or ideas is a means of providing **COHESION** to a text.

result, clause of

These adverbial clauses provide information about the results of the state or action referred to in the main clause:

> *I lost my watch so I was late.*
> *The room was so hot that many people fell asleep.*

Result clauses can be introduced by:

so	*and so*
so that	*so_____that*
such (a)_____that	*in such a way that*

sentence

A unit of language consisting of one or more finite CLAUSES. If a sentence contains just one finite clause it is described as SIMPLE, for example:

> *Simple sentences can be short.*
>
> *After many months of careful negotiations and several journeys to the crash site, the insurance risk assessor and the solicitors representing the victims were able to agree an acceptable compensation package.*

If it contains more than one finite clause, then it is MULTIPLE. The sentences that follow are both multiple.

> *My food arrived and I ate it.*
>
> *After we had negotiated for several months with the insurance risk assessor and had visited the crash site several times, we were able to agree a compensation package which was acceptable to both sides.*

shall

'Shall' is a MODAL AUXILIARY VERB used to refer to possible events in the future:

> *I **shall** be with you shortly.*

See also: WILL, WILL/SHALL

should

'Should' is a MODAL AUXILIARY VERB used to refer to possible events:

> *We **should** be there soon.*

It is also used to express the speaker's opinion of how desirable or obligatory a possible event is:

> *I **should** go over the figures again.*

simple aspect

The simple aspect of the VERB PHRASE is the 'unmarked' form. That is to say that it is not CONTINUOUS, and it is not PERFECT, and is used for all other purposes not covered by those aspects. As a result the SIMPLE PRESENT has a number of widely different applications. These are listed under SIMPLE PRESENT 'TENSE'.

The simple future and simple past are more limited in their applications. The simple past is used to refer to a completed action in the past, or to refer to a sequence of completed actions in the past. The simple future is used to refer to a future action, often showing intention. It is also used to refer to general truths.

simple future 'tense'

This 'tense' is used to refer to a future action, often showing intention.

> Form: *I shall/will walk*
> Example: *He will be there tomorrow.*

This 'tense' is also used to refer to general truths: *In that kind of situation people will think of themselves first.*

See also: TENSE

simple past 'tense'

This 'tense' is used to refer to a completed action in the past.

> Form: *I walked*
> Example: *Darkness fell.*

It is also used to refer to a sequence of completed actions in the past: *They won every match last month.*

See also: TENSE

simple present 'tense'

This tense is used in a variety of ways, the commonest of which are listed below. It has two forms, selected according to the NUMBER and PERSON of the SUBJECT:

	SINGULAR	PLURAL
1st person	I walk	we walk
2nd person	you walk (thou walkest)	you walk
3rd person	he/she/it walks	they walk

Uses:

1. **actions or states that are currently true but have no particular time reference**
   Peter lives in Troon.

2. **habitual actions**
   We visit Manchester once a month.

3. **timeless truths**
   The sun rises in the east.

4. **feelings and thoughts**
   I feel rather sad about that.
   (This is an event that is going on at the time of speaking, but, unusually, does not require the present continuous.)

5. **open conditionals**
   If I see her tomorrow, I'll mention it.

6. **scheduled future actions**
   We go to Edinburgh on Monday, Perth on Tuesday and Inverness on Wednesday.

7. **newspaper headlines**
   PM meets Union bosses

8. **narrative (occasionally)**
   This man goes into a newspaper shop and asks for a cup of tea.

9. **in newspaper and other reviews**
   At this point in the story the hero realises his mistake.

10. **in commentaries**
    Peters crosses, Blake shoots, it's a goal!

simple sentence

A sentence consisting of one clause.
See **SENTENCE**

since

A subordinating conjunction used to introduce two types of adverbial clauses:

- **time**
  I haven't been there since we moved to Sidcup.

- **reason**
  Since Monday is a holiday the meeting has been postponed until Tuesday.

It is also used as a preposition in prepositional phrases of time:

   *I haven't been there **since** 1997.*

split infinitive

When traditionalists say that you should never 'split an infinitive', they mean that you should not place any words between 'to' and the verb stem it accompanies. So, for example, you should not say, *I want to clearly state that I disagree.* Instead you should say, *I want to state clearly that I disagree.* There is no grammatical justification for this 'rule', which derives from the study of Latin, a language in which the infinitive is a single word and is, therefore, impossible to split. In English it is a question of style. Frequently, as in the example above, it isn't necessary to split the infinitive and doing so is rather clumsy. Occasionally, however, it is necessary to split the infinitive, because the intended meaning cannot be conveyed in any other way. For example:

   She's too young to really understand what it was like during the war.

If you place 'really' anywhere else in the sentence, you change the meaning, slightly, but significantly:

   She's too young really to understand what it was like during the war.
   She's too young to understand really what it was like during the war.

See also: INFINITIVE

stem

The base form of the verb, from which, in regular verbs, the other forms are constructed:

stem	walk
infinitive	to walk
present tense	walk/walks
present participle	walking
past tense	walked
past participle	walked

IRREGULAR VERBS depart from this pattern to a greater or lesser extent, but the infinitive and the present participle are always formed from the stem.

structure word

Words which contain no meaning but contribute to the structure of the sentence. If you look them up in a dictionary you will find an explanation of how they are used. They are contrasted with **CONTENT WORDS** which 'contain' some meaning; if you look these up in a dictionary you will find one or more definitions.

subject

The subject of a clause has a number of features. In a statement:

■ It comes at or near the beginning of the clause.

■ It comes before the verb.

In addition it often gives us a good idea of what the sentence is about.

The subject of the sentence frequently determines the form of the verb, which must agree with it in **NUMBER** and **PERSON**. For example:

> *My wife and I are planning a short break in Vienna.* ('we' requires the verb to be 'are')
>
> *The Manager is coming here tomorrow.* ('he/she' requires the verb to be 'is')

The subject can be:
a noun:

> ***Yoga*** *is suitable for people of all ages.*

a pronoun:

> *It benefits both body and mind.*

a noun phrase:

> *Regular exercise is essential for a healthy life.*

certain parts of the verb:

> *To err is human.* (**INFINITIVE**)
> *Walking is better than going by car.* (**GERUND**, or **VERBAL NOUN**)

a noun clause

> *What he said left her puzzled.*

subject complement

Part of a clause that completes the meaning of the subject. In a statement clause it comes after the verb and refers to the same person, thing, or idea as the subject. Examples:

SUBJECT	VERB	SUBJECT COMPLEMENT
The future	seems	uncertain.
Hannah Marsden	will become	our new boss.

A subject complement can be:

■ a noun
  *Cash is **king**.*

■ a pronoun
  *It was **you**!*

■ a numeral
  *I was **third**.*

■ a noun phrase
  *Hannah Marsden will become **our new boss**.*

■ an adjective or adjective phrase
  *The future seems **uncertain**.*

subjective case

See **CASE**

subordinate clause

In a complex sentence there is one main clause and one or more subordinate clauses. The subordinate clauses are dependent, or controlled by, the main clause. Within the grammatical structure of the main clause, subordinate clauses can act as adverbial, subject, object, subject complement, or object complement. For example:

> **What I want to do now** is to have five minutes' rest. (**SUBJECT**)
>
> The letter explained **how the accident happened**. (**OBJECT**)
>
> The problem is **when we should go**. (**SUBJECT COMPLEMENT**)
>
> His loving mother made him **what he is today**. (**OBJECT COMPLEMENT**)
>
> I'll tell you **when we meet**. (**ADVERBIAL**)

In each of these sentences the subordinate clause can be replaced by a phrase or a word, without destroying the grammatical structure of the whole sentence:

> **My only wish** is to have five minutes' rest. (**SUBJECT**)
>
> The letter explained **it**. (**OBJECT**)
>
> The problem is **this**. (**SUBJECT COMPLEMENT**)
>
> His loving mother made him **dependent**. (**OBJECT COMPLEMENT**)
>
> I'll tell you **later**. (**ADVERBIAL**)

If you attempt to replace the main clause with a phrase or word, you destroy the grammatical structure of the sentence.

subordinating conjunction

A conjunction used to introduce a **SUBORDINATE CLAUSE**. Examples are:

when	how	where	why
if	although	unless	since
because	until	so	as

subordinator

See **SUBORDINATING CONJUNCTION**

suffix

Part of the word that comes after the base. In the words that follow the prefixes are printed in bold:

> child**ish**, king**dom**, pictur**esque**

Suffixes change the base into a new word, often of a different word class. So, for example, the noun 'child' becomes an adjective, 'childish'.

superlative

See **COMPARATIVE AND SUPERLATIVE**

syntax

The study of the way in which words are chosen and arranged to form sentences.

tag question

A question 'tagged on' to the end of a statement, generally seeking the listener's agreement. For example:

> *We haven't met before, have we?*
> *You wrote me a letter about this last week, didn't you?*

If the statement contains an **AUXILIARY VERB**, the tag question repeats this, as in the first example. If the statement verb is a simple present, or a simple past, then the tag question uses 'do' or 'did', as in the second example. If the tag question expects the answer 'yes', then it is phrased in the negative (as in example 2); if it expects a negative response, then it is in the positive (as in example 1). In speech it is possible to make tag questions confidently, by giving them a falling tone, or more tentative, by ending with a rising tone.

temporal clause

See **TIME, CLAUSE OF**

tense

In formal grammatical terms, a tense is formed by adding to or changing the verb stem (also known as 'inflecting'). Strictly speaking, therefore, English has two tenses:

> PRESENT TENSE: *I walk, she walks*
> PAST TENSE: *they walked*

The strictly formal definition of tense above is not very helpful when describing how the verb phrase is used to communicate. Many writers use the word 'tense' more loosely to describe the 12 forms of the verb phrase which give information about time and aspect. These 'tenses' are:

	SIMPLE	CONTINUOUS	PERFECT	PERFECT CONTINUOUS
PAST	I walked	I was walking	I had walked	I had been walking
PRESENT	I walk	I am walking	I have walked	I have been walking
FUTURE	I shall walk	I shall be walking	I shall have walked	I shall have been walking

In this book, these are referred to as 'tenses' (in inverted commas) to distinguish them from the two formal tenses, present and past.

that

A word with a number of different uses:

1. **demonstrative pronoun**
   Do you want this book or that?

2. **determiner**
   That seat looks very uncomfortable.

3. **relative pronoun**
   'Dandy Dick' is the play title that I was trying to remember.

4. **subordinating conjunction**
   They told us that we could not stay there.

In uses 3 and 4, 'that' is frequently omitted, especially in informal usage.

that/which/who

These three words are the commonest pronouns used to introduce relative clauses. 'Who' is normally only used to refer to human beings. In formal English it should only be used as the subject of its clause' (see **who/whom** below). 'That' can be used as the subject or the object of the clause, and is quite frequently used to refer to people, most commonly in conversation, especially as the object of the clause ('Who was the man that I saw you with last night?') 'Which' can be the subject or the object of the clause. It is not normally used to refer to people and is used less than 'that' in conversation. It is used much more frequently in formal written English. All three words can introduce RESTRICTIVE RELATIVE CLAUSES. 'That' is not normally used to introduce NON-RESTRICTIVE RELATIVE CLAUSES.

theirs/*their's*

'theirs' is a POSSESSIVE PRONOUN. *'their's'* does not exist.

then

'Then' has three uses:

- **adverb**
  *I didn't know it **then**, but that was the last time I met him.*

- **conjunction**
  *The Prime Minister addressed the house, **then** sat down.*

- (occasionally) **adjective**
  *Mr Blair, the **then** Prime Minister…*

time

Exactly when an action occurs can be shown in English in two ways:

1. **by the form of the verb phrase, the 'TENSE'**

So, for example, 'I shall walk' refers to the future, while 'I walked' refers to the past.

2. **by the use of ADVERBIALS of time**
   For example: *last year, today, next week*

Sometimes, however, 'tense' and time appear to work against each other. The **PRESENT CONTINUOUS** 'tense' can be combined with adverbials of time to refer to the future as well as the present:

> *I am working on Project 'X' at the moment.* (present)
> *I am working on Project 'X' tomorrow.* (future)

The **SIMPLE PRESENT** can be used to refer to the future, to repeated events, to timeless truths, and even to the past:

> *I lift the saucepan off the hob and leave to cool.* (present)
> *They go there every Tuesday.* (repeated)
> *It always rains in Manchester.* (timeless)
> *I fly to Edinburgh tonight.* (future)
> *So he says to me….* (past)

time, adverbial clause of

An **ADVERBIAL CLAUSE** which gives information about **when** an event occurred. Such clauses are sometimes also called 'temporal' clauses. They can be used to describe events that happen:

■ **before the event in the main clause**
   When they received no reply, they knew she was out.

■ **at the same time as the event in the main clause**
   While the match was on, no other work got done.

■ **after the event in the main clause**
   He wrote the letter before he knew all the facts.

Adverbial clauses of time are introduced by the **CONJUNCTIONS**:

> *after, as, before, since, until, when, while*

time, adverbial of

A common use of adverbials is to give information about **when**
events occur. In the following sample sentences, the adverbials are
printed in bold:

> *I only understood the truth **afterwards**.*
> *The accident occurred **at about seven o'clock**.*
> ***After the downpour** it was much less oppressive.*

See also: ADVERBIAL, ADJUNCT

transitive verb

Some MAIN VERBS are followed by an OBJECT and some are not.
Verbs which have an object are described as transitive. Some verbs
almost always take an object. For example: 'hit', 'construct',
'make'. A number of verbs sometimes take an object and
sometimes do not. For example: 'consider', 'write', 'eat'. Verbs that
do not take an object are described as INTRANSITIVE.

uncountable noun

Some common nouns refer to things or ideas that cannot be
counted and therefore do not normally have a plural form. For
example:

> *custard   leather   sadness*

Nouns like these are referred to as 'uncountable' or 'non-count', by
contrast with 'countable' or 'count' nouns.

See also: **fewer/fewest/less/least**

unique

'unique' is a classifying adjective and should not, therefore,
normally be modified. *The Oxford English Dictionary* defines 'unique'
as meaning 'of which there is only one'. As a result, some people
get very irritated when it is graded, as in this phrase from *Country
Life* in 1939:

> *Almost the most unique residential site along the South Coast.*

Others argue that 'unique' as well as meaning 'the only one of its kind' can also mean 'unusual' or 'remarkable'—in which case it can be graded. Indeed, even if you take the stricter view, you must still allow 'unique' to be preceded by 'almost':

> The site was almost unique on the South Coast.

since this simply means 'almost the only one of its kind', which is clearly allowable. As with many things in language use, it is a matter of judgement. If you want to be safe, reserve 'unique' to mean 'the only one of its kind' and never grade it. If you want a similar meaning, with grading, then use an adjective such as 'rare'.

until

This word has two main uses:

- **SUBORDINATING CONJUNCTION** used to introduce an adverbial clause of time:
  > The conflict continued until a peace treaty was signed in 1756.

- **PREPOSITION**
  > The conflict continued until the peace treaty of 1756.

verb

The grammatical term 'verb' is used in two different, but related ways:

- It describes a **WORD CLASS** in the same way as 'noun', 'adjective', and 'preposition' do.

- It describes a part of a clause, in the same way as 'subject' and 'object' do. See **VERB PHRASE**.

Verbs are used:
to express an action

> She **fled**.

to express a state

> She **dreamed**.

to link the subject with a later part of the sentence

> She **was** alone.

Regular verbs have these forms:

> STEM: *walk*
>
> PRESENT TENSE: *walk/walks*
>
> PAST TENSE: *walked*
>
> PRESENT PARTICIPLE: *walking*
>
> PAST PARTICIPLE: *walked*
>
> IRREGULAR VERBS also have these forms but do not follow exactly the pattern of regular verbs.

verb phrase

The verb in a clause is more correctly referred to as the verb phrase, whether it contains one word or more than one. If the verb phrase contains more than one word, all of them will be verbs. If it is one word, then that word is a MAIN VERB. If it is more than one word then it may contain one or more AUXILIARY VERBS.

In a DECLARATORY CLAUSE the verb phrase normally comes after the SUBJECT and before any OBJECT or COMPLEMENT:

SUBJECT	VERB	OBJECT	COMPLEMENT
The music	**continued**.		
It	**was**		*soft.*
It	**improved**	*my mood.*	

The verb phrase is normally FINITE and agrees with the subject in NUMBER and PERSON.

See also: AGREEMENT

verbal noun

A verbal noun, or 'gerund' is the -ing form of the verb used as a noun:

> ***Smoking*** *is forbidden.*
> *I love* ***eating*** *ice cream.*

Because a verbal noun is partly a noun and partly a verb, it can cause problems when preceded by a noun or pronoun. For example, is it:

*She does not like **my** smoking in the house.*
*She does not like **Peter's** smoking in the house.*

or

*She does not like **me** smoking in the house.*
*She does not like **Peter** smoking in the house.*

The former, using the genitive, is accepted by traditionalists but appears to be on the way out. It is advisable to stick to this usage, however, in formal writing and speech, when referring to people.

vocabulary

The words of a language. Also referred to as **LEXIS**.

wh- question

Another name for **QUESTION-WORD QUESTION**.

when

The main uses of 'when' are:

■ **QUESTION WORD**
  When did you last see your father?

■ **relative pronoun**
  The occasion when I remember seeing him was my mother's birthday.

■ **SUBORDINATING CONJUNCTION** introducing a **NOUN CLAUSE**
  She told me when to leave.

where

The main uses of 'where' are:

■ **QUESTION WORD**
  Where shall we go next?

■ **relative pronoun**
  The place where I last saw them was somewhere near Kingston.

■ **SUBORDINATING CONJUNCTION** introducing a **NOUN CLAUSE**
  She told me where to go.

while

A subordinating conjunction used to introduce adverbial clauses of time:

> **While** *this was happening, the children disappeared.*

It also introduced adverbial clauses of concession:

> **While** *I understand your inexperience, I cannot condone incompetence.*

who/whom

Relative clauses are introduced by the relative pronouns *who, whom, whose, which,* and *that.* These can cause some problems, particularly the choice of *who* or *whom.* The traditional rules are these:

1. Use *who* as the subject of the verb.
   Any members **who** *are planning to book courts over the weekend should contact the Secretary.*

2. Use *whom* as the object of the verb.
   Any member **whom** *the Secretary has not contacted by Tuesday should phone her as soon as possible.*

3. Use *whom* after prepositions.
   The person to **whom** *I gave my booking form lost it.*

Increasingly, however, *who* is replacing *whom* in spoken English:

> *Any members* **who** *are planning to book courts over the weekend should contact the Secretary.*
> *Any member* **who** *the Secretary has not contacted by Tuesday should phone her as soon as possible.*
> *The person* **who** *I gave my booking form to lost it.*

On the other hand, most people would still find it strange to hear, *The person to* **who** *I gave my booking form lost it.*

So it is probably acceptable to use *who* as an object in conversation and in informal writing. But *whom* should still be used as an object in formal writing, and *whom* should always be used immediately after a preposition.

Finally, it is worth pointing out that often we use no relative pronoun at all (the 'zero relative') in preference to *whom*:

> *Any member the Secretary has not contacted by Tuesday should phone her as soon as possible.*
>
> *The person I gave my booking form to lost it.*

One way or another, the days of *whom* are probably numbered.

who's/whose

'who's' means 'who is' (*Do you know that woman **who's** standing over there?*)

'whose' means 'of whom' (*The woman **whose** house I'm buying has changed her mind.*)

will

'Will' is a modal auxiliary verb used to refer to possible events in the future:

> *I **will** see you soon.*

See also: SHALL, WILL/SHALL

will/shall

Sometimes it is not clear whether one should use 'shall' or 'will'. The rule of traditional grammar was as follows:

- Normally use 'shall' with 'I' and 'we'. Use 'will' with all other persons.

- Reverse this for emphasis, as in the famous example, 'I will do it and nobody shall help me.'

Increasingly, however, 'will' has become common in all uses. Indeed 'shall' is by far the least common of all the MODAL AUXILIARY VERBS: for every occasion when 'shall' is used in conversation, 'will' is used fourteen times. The only common occurrence of 'shall' with 'I' and 'we' is in questions:

> ***Shall I** do it now?*

The alternative, 'Will I do it now?' is also possible, but in British English tends to be a regional rather than a general usage.

word

The lowest level of language at which we find self-contained units of meaning. There is a lower level, that of MORPHEMES, but these are not always free-standing. Words contribute to the formation of PHRASES, which form CLAUSES, which build into SENTENCES.

would

'Would' is a MODAL AUXILIARY VERB used to refer to a range of possibilities in the future, as is illustrated in the following examples:

> *If I saw her I **would** give her the designs.*
> *I am sure she **would** like them.*

These can be contrasted with:

> *If I see her I **will** give her the designs.*
> *I am sure she **will** like them.*

The versions using 'will' are more open: the event may or may not happen. Those using 'would' seem less open and less likely, although still possible.

Other uses of 'would' are:

- **habitual actions in the past**:
  *Every week they **would** play a round of golf together.*

- **actions that are regarded as typical**:
  *He **would** have the last word!*

yes/no question

A question expecting the answers 'Yes' or 'No'. For example:

> *Are you going to the match tomorrow?*

AskOxford.COM
Oxford Dictionaries Passionate about language

For more information about the background to Oxford Quotations and Language Reference Dictionaries, and much more about Oxford's commitment to language exploration, why not visit the world's largest language learning site, www.AskOxford.com

Passionate about English?

What were the original 'brass monkeys'? **Ask**Oxford.COM

How do new words enter the dictionary? **Ask**Oxford.COM

How is 'whom' used? **Ask**Oxford.COM

Who said, 'For also knowledge itself is power?' **Ask**Oxford.COM

How can I improve my writing? **Ask**Oxford.COM

If you have a query about the English language, want to look up a word, need some help with your writing skills, are curious about how dictionaries are made, or simply have some time to learn about the language, bypass the rest and ask the experts at www.AskOxford.com.

Passionate about language?

If you want to find out about writing in French, German, Spanish, or Italian, improve your listening and speaking skills, learn about other cultures, access resources for language students, or gain insider travel tips from those **Ask**Oxford.COM in the know, ask the experts at

OXFORD

Oxford Paperback Reference

The Concise Oxford Dictionary of English Etymology
T. F. Hoad

A wealth of information about our language and its history, this reference source provides over 17,000 entries on word origins.

'A model of its kind'

Daily Telegraph

A Dictionary of Euphemisms
R. W. Holder

This hugely entertaining collection draws together euphemisms from all aspects of life: work, sexuality, age, money, and politics.

Review of the previous edition
'This ingenious collection is not only very funny but extremely instructive too'

Iris Murdoch

The Oxford Dictionary of Slang
John Ayto

Containing over 10,000 words and phrases, this is the ideal reference for those interested in the more quirky and unofficial words used in the English language.

'hours of happy browsing for language lovers'

Observer

Oxford Companions

'Opening such books is like sitting down with a knowledgeable friend. Not a bore or a know-all, but a genuinely well-informed chum ... So far so splendid.'

Sunday Times [of *The Oxford Companion to Shakespeare*]

For well over 60 years Oxford University Press has been publishing Companions that are of lasting value and interest, each one not only a comprehensive source of reference, but also a stimulating guide, mentor, and friend. There are between 40 and 60 Oxford Companions available at any one time, ranging from music, art, and literature to history, warfare, religion, and wine.

Titles include:

The Oxford Companion to English Literature
Edited by Margaret Drabble
'No guide could come more classic.'

Malcolm Bradbury, *The Times*

The Oxford Companion to Music
Edited by Alison Latham
'probably the best one-volume music reference book going'

Times Educational Supplement

The Oxford Companion to Western Art
Edited by Hugh Brigstocke
'more than meets the high standard set by the growing number of Oxford Companions'

Contemporary Review

The Oxford Companion to Food
Alan Davidson
'the best food reference work ever to appear in the English language'

New Statesman

The Oxford Companion to Wine
Edited by Jancis Robinson
'the greatest wine book ever published'

Washington Post

OXFORD

Great value ebooks from Oxford!

An ever-increasing number of Oxford subject reference dictionaries, English and bilingual dictionaries, and English language reference titles are available as ebooks.

All Oxford ebooks are available in the award-winning Mobipocket Reader format, compatible with most current handheld systems, including Palm, Pocket PC/Windows CE, Psion, Nokia, SymbianOS, Franklin eBookMan, and Windows. Some are also available in MS Reader and Palm Reader formats.

Priced on a par with the print editions, Oxford ebooks offer dictionary-specific search options making information retrieval quick and easy.

For further information and a full list of Oxford ebooks please visit: www.askoxford.com/shoponline/ebooks/

OXFORD

Oxford Paperback Reference

The Kings of Queens of Britain
John Cannon and Anne Hargreaves

A detailed, fully-illustrated history ranging from mythical and pre-conquest rulers to the present House of Windsor, featuring regional maps and genealogies.

A Dictionary of Dates
Cyril Leslie Beeching

Births and deaths of the famous, significant and unusual dates in history – this is an entertaining guide to each day of the year.

'a dipper's blissful paradise ... Every single day of the year, plus an index of birthdays and chronologies of scientific developments and world events.'

Observer

A Dictionary of British History
Edited by John Cannon

An invaluable source of information covering the history of Britain over the past two millennia. Over 3,600 entries written by more than 100 specialist contributors.

Review of the parent volume
'the range is impressive ... truly (almost) all of human life is here'
Kenneth Morgan, *Observer*

OXFORD

Oxford Paperback Reference

The Concise Oxford Dictionary of Art & Artists
Ian Chilvers

Based on the highly praised *Oxford Dictionary of Art*, over 2,500 up-to-date entries on painting, sculpture, and the graphic arts.

'the best and most inclusive single volume available, immensely useful and very well written'

Marina Vaizey, *Sunday Times*

The Concise Oxford Dictionary of Art Terms
Michael Clarke

Written by the Director of the National Gallery of Scotland, over 1,800 entries cover periods, styles, materials, techniques, and foreign terms.

A Dictionary of Architecture
James Stevens Curl

Over 5,000 entries and 250 illustrations cover all periods of Western architectural history.

'splendid ... you can't have a more concise, entertaining, and informative guide to the words of architecture'

Architectural Review

'excellent, and amazing value for money ... by far the best thing of its kind'

Professor David Walker

OXFORD

Oxford Paperback Reference

The Concise Oxford Companion to English Literature
Margaret Drabble and Jenny Stringer

Based on the best-selling *Oxford Companion to English Literature*, this is
an indispensable guide to all aspects of English literature.

Review of the parent volume
'a magisterial and monumental achievement'

Literary Review

The Concise Oxford Companion to Irish Literature
Robert Welch

From the ogam alphabet developed in the 4th century to Roddy Doyle,
this is a comprehensive guide to writers, works, topics, folklore, and
historical and cultural events.

Review of the parent volume
'Heroic volume ... It surpasses previous exercises of similar nature in the
richness of its detail and the ecumenism of its approach.'

Times Literary Supplement

A Dictionary of Shakespeare
Stanley Wells

Compiled by one of the best-known international authorities on the
playwright's works, this dictionary offers up-to-date information on all
aspects of Shakespeare, both in his own time and in later ages.

OXFORD

Oxford Paperback Reference

Concise Medical Dictionary

Over 10,000 clear entries covering all the major medical and surgical specialities make this one of our best-selling dictionaries.

'"No home should be without one" certainly applies to this splendid medical dictionary'

Journal of the Institute of Health Education

'An extraordinary bargain'

New Scientist

'Excellent layout and jargon-free style'

Nursing Times

A Dictionary of Nursing

Comprehensive coverage of the ever-expanding vocabulary of the nursing professions. Features over 10,000 entries written by medical and nursing specialists.

An A-Z of Medicinal Drugs

Over 4,000 entries cover the full range of over-the-counter and prescription medicines available today. An ideal reference source for both the patient and the medical professional.

OXFORD

Oxford Paperback Reference

The Concise Oxford Dictionary of Quotations
Edited by Elizabeth Knowles

Based on the highly acclaimed *Oxford Dictionary of Quotations*, this paperback edition maintains its extensive coverage of literary and historical quotations, and contains completely up-to-date material. A fascinating read and an essential reference tool.

The Oxford Dictionary of Humorous Quotations
Edited by Ned Sherrin

From the sharply witty to the downright hilarious, this sparkling collection will appeal to all senses of humour.

Quotations by Subject
Edited by Susan Ratcliffe

A collection of over 7,000 quotations, arranged thematically for easy look-up. Covers an enormous range of nearly 600 themes from 'The Internet' to 'Parliament'.

The Concise Oxford Dictionary of Phrase and Fable
Edited by Elizabeth Knowles

Provides a wealth of fascinating and informative detail for over 10,000 phrases and allusions used in English today. Find out about anything from the 'Trojan house' to 'ground zero'.

OXFORD

Oxford Paperback Reference

The Concise Oxford Dictionary of World Religions
Edited by John Bowker

Over 8,200 entries containing unrivalled coverage of all the major world religions, past and present.

'covers a vast range of topics ... is both comprehensive and reliable'

The Times

The Oxford Dictionary of Saints
David Farmer

From the famous to the obscure, over 1,400 saints are covered in this acclaimed dictionary.

'an essential reference work'

Daily Telegraph

The Concise Oxford Dictionary of the Christian Church
E. A. Livingstone

This indispensable guide contains over 5,000 entries and provides full coverage of theology, denominations, the church calendar, and the Bible.

'opens up the whole of Christian history, now with a wider vision than ever'

Robert Runcie, former Archbishop of Canterbury

More Literature titles from OUP

Shakespeare: An Oxford Guide
Stanley Wells and Lena Cowen Orlin

This comprehensive guide to Shakespeare comprises over 40 specially commissioned essays by an outstanding team of contemporary Shakespeare scholars.

Literature in the Modern World
Dennis Walder

A unique perspective for students on literary studies from the 1920s to the present day.

The Poetry Handbook
John Lennard

A lucid and entertaining guide to the poet's craft, and an invaluable introduction to practical criticism.

**VISIT THE HIGHER EDUCATION LITERATURE WEB SITE AT
www.oup.com/uk/best.textbooks/literature**

OXFORD

More Art Reference from Oxford

The Grove Dictionary of Art

The 34 volumes of *The Grove Dictionary of Art* provide unrivalled coverage of
the visual arts from Asia, Africa, the Americas, Europe, and the Pacific, from
prehistory to the present day.

'succeeds in performing the most difficult of balancing acts, satisfying
specialists while ... remaining accessible to the general reader'

The Times

The Grove Dictionary of Art – Online
www.groveart.com

This immense cultural resource is now available online. Updated regularly, it
includes recent developments in the art world as well as the latest art
scholarship.

'a mammoth one-stop site for art-related information'

Antiques Magazine

The Oxford History of Western Art
Edited by Martin Kemp

From Classical Greece to postmodernism, *The Oxford History of Western Art* is
an authoritative and stimulating overview of the development of visual
culture in the West over the last 2,700 years.

'here is a work that will permanently alter the face of art history ... a hugely
ambitious project successfully achieved'

The Times

The Oxford Dictionary of Art
Edited by Ian Chilvers

The Oxford Dictionary of Art is an authoritative guide to the art of the western
world, ranging across painting, sculpture, drawing, and the applied arts.

'the best and most inclusive single-volume available'

Marina Vaizey, *Sunday Times*

Oxford Paperback Reference

The Oxford Dictionary of Dance
Debra Craine and Judith Mackrell

Over 2,500 entries on everything from hip-hop to classical ballet, covering dancers, dance styles, choreographers and composers, techniques, companies, and productions.

'A must-have volume ... impressively thorough'

Margaret Reynolds, *The Times*

Who's Who in Opera
Joyce Bourne

Covering operas, operettas, roles, perfomances, and well-known personalities.

'a generally scrupulous and scholarly book'

Opera

The Concise Oxford Dictionary of Music
Michael Kennedy

The most comprehensive, authoritative, and up-to-date dictionary of music available in paperback.

'clearly the best around ... the dictionary that everyone should have'

Literary Review